Praise for

Oh No He Didn't!

Murphy, an attorney specializing in women's rights and violence against women and children, focuses her book on innovative and genius women throughout history and the men who took credit for their contributions to physics, astronomy, economics, the arts, and architecture. Utilizing archival material and other research, Murphy draws from her own personal experiences too; a professor and then a student plagiarized her work. She writes with a jaded, edgy humor in a style that is bold and relatable without sacrificing historical accuracy or seriousness. This exceptional book's stories of plagiarism showcase persistence and the insidious and enduring ways in which sexism informs and shapes the contemporary world. Murphy will motivate readers to challenge stereotypes.

—*Library Journal*

I see the spirit of my great-great-grandmother Elizabeth Cady Stanton in all these women, and I hear her voice in the words of Wendy Murphy not only in this book but in her tireless fight for the Equal Rights Amendment. Her leadership, brilliance, and fierce refusal to compromise or accept less than full equality for women are unrivaled. Elizabeth Cady Stanton and Alice Paul are so proud as we stand on their shoulders.

—**Coline Jenkins,**
great-great-granddaughter
of Elizabeth Cady Stanton

OH NO HE DIDN'T!

OH NO HE DIDN'T!

Brilliant Women and the Men Who Took Credit for Their Work

Wendy J. Murphy, JD

Published by Cynren Press
Chester County, Pennsylvania
http://www.cynren.com/

First published 2024

Printed in the United States of America

ISBN-13: 978-1-947976-47-4 (pbk)
ISBN-13: 978-1-947976-44-3 (ebk)

Library of Congress Control Number: 2023943596

Cover design by Kevin Barrett Kane

To my amazing children,
Grant, Taylor, Reed, Cameron, and Brit.
They would have stood up fearlessly for these women.
And to my first grandchild, Milo,
who is being raised to care.

Contents

Introduction

WE ALL HAVE A STORY

Have you ever come up with an idea, only to have someone else claim it as their own? How did that make you feel? Did you speak up? If not, why? If so, what steps did you take to remedy the situation? Were they successful? Was it worth the effort? I've had many such experiences—some I complained about; others I did not. One of my law students cut a few pages from an article of mine and pasted it into his final paper, without attribution. I was furious and, frankly, shocked that a student would be dumb enough to plagiarize his professor, but then I found out that he had taken it from another lawyer who had stolen it from me, so he didn't even know he was plagiarizing me because he was plagiarizing another plagiarist.

Another incident happened when I was working for NBC and a colleague tried to take credit for a news scoop I got during the so-called Nanny Trial in the mid-1990s. A British au pair named Louise Woodward was convicted of murdering baby Matthew Eappen by shaking him and fracturing his skull. Her well-funded defense team made a global spectacle of the trial and had asked the judge to reduce the verdict from murder to manslaughter. Along with dozens of others in the media who were covering the case, I was sitting outside the courthouse awaiting the judge's decision.

My job as a legal analyst for NBC was to explain issues to viewers, not necessarily report on breaking news, but because I was also a former prosecutor who had worked in the same office where Woodward was on trial, I had contacts I could call for information. This was important because every news station wanted to be the first to announce the judge's decision, and I had a friend who was working on the case.

The judge said he would release his ruling by posting it on the internet, but the technology didn't work, so my friend called me to let me know that the judge had reduced the verdict to manslaughter. I was in an NBC Town Car when I got the call, so I hung up quickly and ran toward the outdoor set where cameras were already rolling, yelling, "He reduced the verdict! He reduced the verdict!" Another legal analyst who was already on-set, well-known TV lawyer Dan Abrams, was sitting in front of the camera when he heard me yell the news from ten yards away. He turned to the camera to announce the judge's decision, without mentioning that I was the one who had gotten the information. By the time I got into my chair and put my microphone on, nobody wanted to talk to me because they assumed Abrams was the one who had gotten the scoop.

When we finally broke for a commercial, Abrams walked away from the set without saying anything. A few minutes later, he came back and asked me how I had gotten the information. He was on the phone with NBC management, and they wanted to know how he found out about the judge's decision. He angrily demanded that I tell him my source so he could answer the boss's questions. I told him if they needed to know, they could call me themselves. He was furious, spitting his words and insisting that I tell him because he was senior to me. I smirked and walked away. NBC brass then called me, and I told them the truth: that I had a friend in the office who called me after a computer snafu prevented the judge from announcing his decision via the internet. Lucky for me, the *Boston Globe* wrote a story the next day explaining that I was the one who broke the story.

I haven't always been treated unfairly as a woman, though the times when I was were pretty bad. I was forced to bring my two-day-old baby to the Supreme Judicial Court of

Massachusetts to argue a case because a judge didn't think me giving birth was important enough to accommodate. The court had offered August 9 or 22 as possible hearing dates, and I quickly replied that I was scheduled to give birth to my fifth child on August 13 and could only make the August 9 date. My two opponent lawyers, both men, said they were unavailable on the ninth, so the hearing was scheduled for the twenty-second to accommodate them. When my baby didn't arrive by August 19, I asked my doctor to induce me that evening, so I could get out of the hospital on the twenty-first and get to court the following morning. Luckily things went well, and I made it to court, exhausted and still in my maternity clothes, with my newborn in tow. A local reporter delighted in writing about the court's disrespect for my situation, captioning his story "Lawyer to Stand and Deliver in Court." The court's horrendous treatment of me led to enormous media coverage, which helped my client. I won the case, and a violent rapist who had evaded the legal system for fourteen years was finally sent to prison.

In another case, a judge refused to give me a fifteen-minute morning break to breastfeed my newborn, even though he had ordered me to try the case in the middle of my maternity leave. In fact, the trial was supposed to begin when I was eight and a half months' pregnant, but the judge granted my male opponent a one-month delay because my bulging belly would prejudice the jury in my favor. I returned a month later with my newborn daughter, Taylor, and my mother, who would care for her in a private courthouse room while I tried the case. I asked the judge for a morning break so that I could nurse my baby, but he said, "We don't take breaks for that." So I sent the baby home with my mother. My breasts were extremely sore by the time I got home after being on trial all day; Taylor couldn't even nurse properly because my nipples had stretched flat. My boss at the time wanted me to file a complaint against the judge, but I declined out of fear he would retaliate against me in other cases. I regret that decision.

For the most part, I have been treated fairly. Early in my career, I even won Lawyer of the Year in Massachusetts, alongside my husband and eight other lawyers. I won because I overturned a terrible decision the Supreme Judicial Court had handed down years earlier, requiring rape victims to turn over all confidential files, even if they were decades old and irrelevant. Medical, counseling, and school records dating back to a victim's childhood were all fair game. Forcing victims to choose between dignity and justice was unconscionable, and I wanted to challenge the law, but no lawyer had ever done what I was planning to do, and it was risky. I wanted the director of a rape crisis center to disobey a judge's order requiring her to turn over a victim's counseling file. She would be held in contempt and maybe incarcerated, but it would give me the right to file an appeal and overturn the law on the grounds that it violated victims' constitutionally protected privacy rights. The director was terrified of going to jail but angry enough to risk her freedom. She allowed herself to be held in contempt. I filed an appeal, and we won a landmark ruling that overturned the law.

My husband won Lawyer of the Year for a different reason. He had litigated a high-profile class action case and won an important verdict on behalf of the public interest. When our faces appeared alongside full-page stories about our accomplishments in the Lawyer of the Year edition of *Massachusetts Lawyers Weekly*, some people cried foul because they thought it was unfair for a husband and wife to be honored at the same time. The editors at *Lawyers Weekly* had to write a follow-up piece explaining that they'd had no idea we were married. Even during the long interviews they did with each of us, they did not figure out that we were married because neither of us mentioned it and we did not have the same last name. When the editor called me to tell me about the controversy, he said if he had known we were married, he would not have honored both of us. I dreaded his next sentence, as I was sure he was going to say that I would have been left behind, but instead he said, "We would have cut your husband, as he was further down the list of nominees and your work was more clever."

Women don't always lose out to men, and it's important to talk about the times when we do prevail based on merit. But more often than not, we get second place when we deserve first, or we get ignored, cheated, and disrespected, and we say nothing because we think it isn't worth the effort. Just a few years ago, an attorney named Lance Houston promised to pay me and a male lawyer $100 each to give a talk about new Title IX regulations. After my presentation, I asked for payment, and he told me the check was in the mail. It never arrived, though he did pay the man who presented with me. He didn't care that he'd breached our agreement. He was an entitled man who felt comfortable disrespecting a woman. I insulted him publicly and did what I could, but what difference did it make?

My personal experiences are trivial compared to what the women in this book went through, but we all have stories, and they need to be told. If we stay quiet, we're part of the problem.

In science, the phenomenon of men taking credit for women's work is so common that it has a name: the Matilda Effect. It was coined in 1993 by science historian Margaret Rossiter in honor of suffragist and abolitionist Matilda Joslyn Gage, who, in 1870, wrote an essay describing how women scientists were not getting the credit they deserved. Women in all fields experience some version of the Matilda Effect, even when they perform at the highest professional levels. Only 60 women have won Nobel Prizes, compared to 898 men. In architecture, only 7 percent of Pritzker Prize winners have been women. And though women win only slightly fewer literary prizes compared to men, a massive gender disparity emerges when the topic of prize-winning books is examined. Novels with a female main character are much less likely to win than novels in which the main character is a man. Between 2000 and 2015, no book-length work about a woman or with a female-driven narrative won a Pulitzer Prize.

Unfair treatment of women is hard to see sometimes, especially when so many are highly accomplished and doing well. But we know that women as a class suffer terrible injustices, and we know why: the US Constitution has never granted women full legal equality, which means no laws must, as a constitutional matter, be applied equally to women. This problem is not unique to the United States. In 2020 the

United Nations released a report on the global status of women and concluded that "no country has achieved gender equality." Without equality, women suffer unfair treatment in all areas of life, public and private, not only in terms of men taking credit for their work but also in the form of unequal pay, pregnancy discrimination, and disproportionately high rates of rape, domestic abuse, and femicide.

It would help if the issue of women's inequality were taught in schools, but it is not part of any mandatory curriculum. This makes it harder for people to understand why men develop a sense of entitlement that seems at once unfair and inevitable. President Bill Clinton made this clear many years ago when a reporter asked him why he took advantage of Monica Lewinsky—he did it because he "could."

The flip side of men feeling entitled to take credit for women's work is women allowing them to do it. This was especially true years ago, when women rightly believed that letting a man take credit was the only way to have their work respected. But even today, women seem passively resigned to male superiority. For example, most women take their husbands' last names when they get married, even though this practice is steeped in an offensive legal doctrine known as coverture, which subsumed married women's legal existence under that of their husbands. Women who keep their original surnames aren't really addressing the problem, because they usually have their fathers' last names. I intentionally refer to the women in this book by their first names as a way of liberating them from this unfortunate history. I'm not sure it helps, or what the solution is, but it's a problem that women's identities are still determined by their relationships to men.

While we continue to fight for equality, women must remember that regardless of our different races, social classes, sexual orientations, religions, and ethnicities, we suffer the same when we suffer as women. When one sexual assault happens, it hurts all of us. When one woman isn't paid fairly, it legitimizes unfair pay for all women. We also benefit as a class when a woman achieves success in a male-dominated field. In 2019 a woman was awarded the prestigious Abel Prize in mathematics; in 2020 a woman was elected vice president of the United

States; in 2021 a woman was appointed director-general of the World Trade Organization; in 2022 a woman became president of a National Football League team; in 2023 an all-women crew of firefighters ran a firehouse. These accomplishments don't change the law, but they help by changing cultural expectations and ideas about women's roles in society. As the saying goes, "if you can see it, you can be it."

The day will come when there are no more firsts for women, but even then, we will continue to suffer injustices big and small so long as we remain unequal. Keep this in mind as you read these stories, and imagine how things might have turned out differently if these women had had basic legal equality when men took credit for their work.

1

HE SAID HE DISCOVERED CLIMATE CHANGE, BUT HE LIED

The category is "Women in Science." The answer? "Eunice Foote." The question? "Who discovered global warming?" In March 2023 a contestant on *Jeopardy* got this one right—but for the previous century and a half, history had it wrong. Nobody knew that Eunice Foote discovered climate change because a man named John Tyndall falsely claimed that he'd made the discovery, and everyone believed him.

Eunice was born Eunice Newton on July 17, 1819, in Goshen, Connecticut. One of twelve children of Thirza and Isaac Newton (reportedly a distant relative of Sir Isaac Newton), Eunice was raised in a family that valued education for girls as much as for boys. In 1836 she enrolled at the Troy Female Seminary, a school founded in 1821 by Emma Hart Willard as the first college in the United States to offer an education to women comparable to that which was offered to men. Willard believed that educating women was even more important than giving them the vote, so she designed Troy as a school where women could learn all disciplines, including science and math.

Troy had a laboratory where students could conduct their own experiments, which was very unusual for the time. This

Artist's rendition of Eunice Foote. Drawing by Carlyn Iverson, NOAA Climate.gov.

enabled Eunice to learn the scientific method and gain hands-on experience. Women at Troy were also allowed to study alongside men at a nearby technological college, now known as Rensselaer Polytechnic Institute, so Eunice took science courses there too.

Eunice studied at Troy for several years and wanted to be a scientist, but women were not welcome in the profession. She married a mathematician and judge named Elisha Foote in 1841 and settled in Seneca Falls, New York. The couple shared a passion for science and, in 1842, invented a thermostatically controlled cooking stove. They applied for a patent in Elisha's name only, because married women had no rights of their own, which meant that Eunice could not go to court and defend herself if her invention were stolen.

Seneca Falls was a hotbed of social activism in the mid-1800s. Eunice and Elisha were neighbors of famed suffragist Elizabeth Cady Stanton, who had also studied at Troy. Elizabeth's father, a well-known judge named Daniel Cady, had trained Elisha in law.

Eunice and Elizabeth worked together on women's rights and served on the editorial committee for the historic 1848 Seneca Falls Convention, where the Declaration of Sentiments was read. It was a powerful list of grievances that condemned the social, political, and legal subjugation of women in

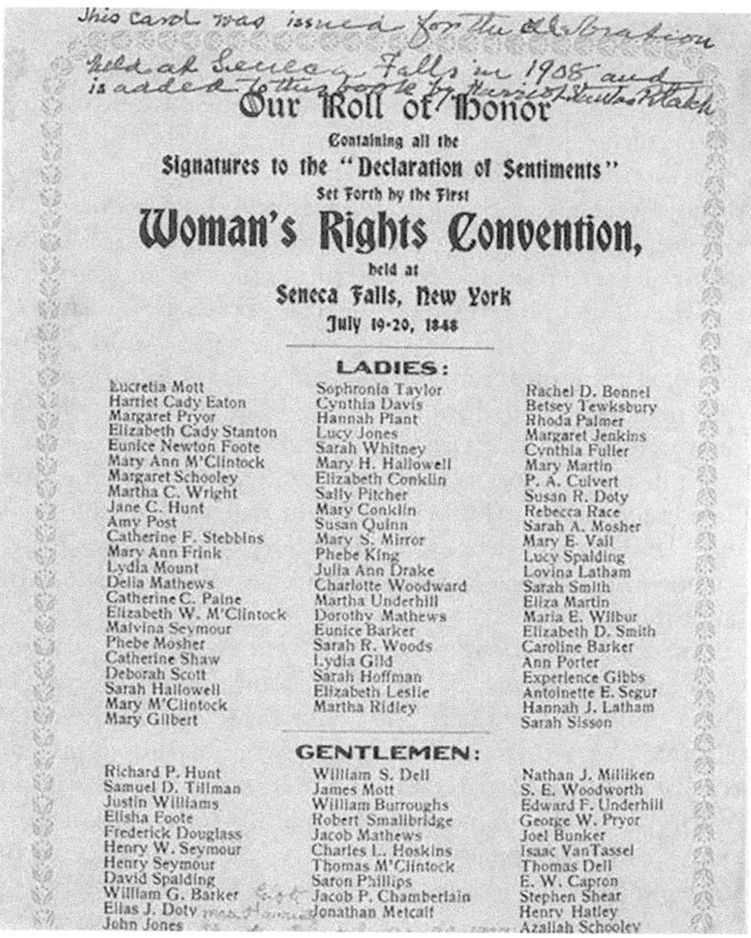

This card was issued for the celebration held at Seneca Falls in 1908 and is added to this book by Harriot Stanton Blatch

Our Roll of Honor

Containing all the

Signatures to the "Declaration of Sentiments"

Set Forth by the First

Woman's Rights Convention,

held at

Seneca Falls, New York

July 19-20, 1848

LADIES:

Lucretia Mott
Harriet Cady Eaton
Margaret Pryor
Elizabeth Cady Stanton
Eunice Newton Foote
Mary Ann M'Clintock
Margaret Schooley
Martha C. Wright
Jane C. Hunt
Amy Post
Catherine F. Stebbins
Mary Ann Frink
Lydia Mount
Delia Mathews
Catherine C. Paine
Elizabeth W. M'Clintock
Malvina Seymour
Phebe Mosher
Catherine Shaw
Deborah Scott
Sarah Hallowell
Mary M'Clintock
Mary Gilbert

Sophronia Taylor
Cynthia Davis
Hannah Plant
Lucy Jones
Sarah Whitney
Mary H. Hallowell
Elizabeth Conklin
Sally Pitcher
Mary Conklin
Susan Quinn
Mary S. Mirror
Phebe King
Julia Ann Drake
Charlotte Woodward
Martha Underhill
Dorothy Mathews
Eunice Barker
Sarah R. Woods
Lydia Gild
Sarah Hoffman
Elizabeth Leslie
Martha Ridley

Rachel D. Bonnel
Betsey Tewksbury
Rhoda Palmer
Margaret Jenkins
Cynthia Fuller
Mary Martin
P. A. Culvert
Susan R. Doty
Rebecca Race
Sarah A. Mosher
Mary E. Vail
Lucy Spalding
Lovina Latham
Sarah Smith
Eliza Martin
Maria E. Wilbur
Elizabeth D. Smith
Caroline Barker
Ann Porter
Experience Gibbs
Antoinette E. Segur
Hannah J. Latham
Sarah Sisson

GENTLEMEN:

Richard P. Hunt
Samuel D. Tillman
Justin Williams
Elisha Foote
Frederick Douglass
Henry W. Seymour
Henry Seymour
David Spalding
William G. Barker
Elias J. Doty
John Jones

William S. Dell
James Mott
William Burroughs
Robert Smallbridge
Jacob Mathews
Charles L. Hoskins
Thomas M'Clintock
Saron Phillips
Jacob P. Chamberlain
Jonathan Metcalf

Nathan J. Milliken
S. E. Woodworth
Edward F. Underhill
George W. Pryor
Joel Bunker
Isaac VanTassel
Thomas Dell
E. W. Capron
Stephen Shear
Henry Hatley
Azaliah Schooley

The 1848 Declaration of Sentiments, signed by Eunice and her husband, Elisha. Courtesy https://pbs.twimg.com/media/CKXzBSKWwAEzQT8.jpg. Reproduced under a Creative Commons Attribution-Share Alike 4.0 International license, https://creativecommons.org/licenses/by-sa/4.0/deed.en.

America and declared, in stark contrast to the Declaration of Independence, that "all men *and women* are created equal." Eunice, Elizabeth, and their husbands all signed the declaration, along with ninety-six other men and women.

While fighting for women's rights, Eunice also worked as an amateur scientist; she even built a lab in her home. In 1856 she designed an experiment to see how the sun's heat affects different gases in the atmosphere. Of the three gases she tested—carbon dioxide, air, and hydrogen—Eunice discovered that carbon dioxide trapped the most heat and needed the longest time away from the sun to cool. In her findings Eunice wrote, "The highest effect of the sun's rays, I have found to be in carbonic acid gas [carbon dioxide]." She explained, "An atmosphere of that gas would give to our earth a high temperature; and if as some suppose, at one period of its history the air had mixed with it a larger proportion than at present, an increased temperature from its own action as well as from increased weight must have necessarily resulted." In other words, Eunice discovered that carbon dioxide in the atmosphere causes Earth to become hotter—a phenomenon known today as the greenhouse effect.

Eunice wrote a paper about her experiment, and it was presented on August 23, 1856, at the tenth annual meeting of the prestigious American Association for the Advancement of Science (AAAS), but not by Eunice. Women did not present research at AAAS, so a renowned male scientist by the name of Joseph Henry, then head of the Smithsonian Institution, read Eunice's paper for her. Henry wanted science to be more welcoming to women, so he took advantage of the opportunity to make a statement about their abilities, saying, "Science is of no country and of no sex."

Eunice's paper was published later that same year in the highly respected *American Journal of Science and Arts* (*AJSA*). It was the first time a woman's research paper in physics was published in a peer-reviewed scientific journal.

Summaries of Eunice's paper were subsequently published in 1856 and 1857 in several other scientific journals and magazines in the United States and abroad, including in the September 13, 1856, edition of *Scientific American*. Editors wrote, "This we are happy to say has been done by a lady," and "The experiments of Mrs. Foote afford abundant evidence of the ability of woman to investigate any subject with originality and precision."

On the Heat in the Sun's Rays. 377

ART. XXX.—*On the Heat in the Sun's Rays;* by ELISHA FOOTE.

(Read before the Amer. Association for the Advancement of Science, Aug. 23, 1856.)

THE experiments here detailed were instituted for the purpose of investigating the heat in the Sun's rays.

Two instruments have been used for this purpose. One was Leslie's differential thermometer. Both bulbs of it were blackened by holding them in the smoke of burning pitch. When experimenting one was shaded, the other was exposed to the direct action of the sun's rays; and as both were thus equally subject to all other influences, the result was not affected by them.

Generally, however, I have found it more convenient to use two mercurial thermometers, and note their difference. Two small and very delicate instruments were procured as nearly alike as possible. The stems of both were attached to the same plate about two inches apart, and the scales were marked upon it in juxtaposition, so that the eye could see the indications of both at the same time. Both bulbs were blackened as in the other instrument. It was used in the same manner. The temperatures in the sun and in the shade were noted, and their difference was taken as equivalent to the indications of the differential thermometer.

The question that first arises is, does the difference between the shaded and exposed bulbs afford a correct measure of the heat in the sun's rays? To this point I would ask attention before proceeding to the experiment.

The theory of the differential thermometer was accurately investigated by Leslie. In one of the foci of two parabolic reflectors he placed a tin canister which was heated or cooled by putting in liquids of different temperatures or frigorific mixtures. In the other, the heat was received on one of the bulbs of his differential thermometer: and under all circumstances, the indications of the instrument were found to be accurately proportional to the differences between the temperatures of the canister and those of the surrounding air.

I have varied these experiments by keeping the canister at the uniform heat of boiling water in different temperatures of the air, and by substituting other sources of heat, and have always found the results to accord with those obtained by the distinguished philosopher to whom I have referred.

The principles of radiation lead to the same result; for while the differential thermometer receives heat from the canister, it at the same time radiates it to surrounding bodies, and that in pro-

SECOND SERIES, VOL. XXII, NO. 66.—NOV., 1856.
48

378 *On the Heat in the Sun's Rays.*

portion or nearly so to the difference between its temperature and that of the medium in which it is placed.

I regard it therefore as well established that the differential thermometer affords a correct measurement of the *differences* between the heat of the canister and that of the surrounding air. These differences may evidently be varied in two ways: by changing either—

1st. The heat of the canister; or—

2dly. The temperature of the air.

An increase or diminution in the heat of the canister would directly increase or diminish the differences; whilst an increase in the temperature of the air would diminish the difference until an equality between the two was obtained. If the temperature of the air were uniform and the changes were those of the canister alone, the instrument measuring the differences would correctly indicate those changes. But if the heat of the canister were uniform and that of the air were varied, then would the instrument equally indicate those changes, but in a contrary direction. In case the heat of both the canister and the air was varied at the same time, if we knew the change in one and its effects upon the instrument, we could *easily* deduce the changes in the other. Suppose, for example, an increase of ten degrees on the scale of the instrument and an elevation of five degrees in the temperature of the air; the effect of the latter having been to depress the thermometer five degrees, and the canister having not only overcome that effect but increased the indications ten degrees, the sum of the two or fifteen degrees would be the real change which had taken place in the heat of the canister. Had there been a depression in the temperature of the air, it obviously should be subtracted from the indications of the instrument to obtain the desired measurement.

It is upon these principles that I have applied the differential thermometer to measure the comparative heat in the sun's rays. One of its bulbs received their direct action in the same way that it received the rays proceeding from the canister. The temperature of the air was at the same time obtained by a common thermometer. An increase was added to, and a diminution subtracted from, the indications of the instrument to obtain the real changes in the heat of the rays proceeding from the sun.

My first experiment was of the simplest kind. It was a winter's day. The differential thermometer was placed on the outside of a window where the temperature was below the freezing point. The effect measured by the scale (which merely divided the stem into equal parts) was 58°. It was then placed on the inside of the window where the temperature was about 70°, and to my surprise the effect rose to 115°. The experiment was many times repeated with similar results, although varying

The first two pages of Eunice's paper "Circumstances Affecting the Heat of the Sun's Rays." From the *American Journal of Science and Arts* 22 (Nov. 1856).

In 1857 Eunice completed another experiment, this time on static electricity. Again, her findings were presented at the AAAS annual meeting, and again, her paper was published in the *AJSA*.

By 1857, Eunice had chalked up a lot of firsts. She had attended the first college to offer women equal educational opportunities, she was the first woman to have had a scientific paper presented at the prestigious AAAS conference, and she was the first woman to have had a research paper on physics published in a peer-reviewed scientific journal. But none of this was enough for a man named John Tyndall. In 1859, Tyndall conducted an experiment confirming Eunice's 1856 discovery of the greenhouse effect, but he did not cite or credit Eunice's work in his paper. In fact, he claimed to be the first person to recognize how the sun's heat affects different gases in the atmosphere, saying, "Nothing so far as I am aware has been published on the transmission of radiant heat through gaseous bodies."

Tyndall protested too much. Plenty of evidence shows that he knew about Eunice's work.

For starters, Tyndall's scientific work before 1859 had nothing to do with the sun's heat and atmospheric gases. He focused on this topic only after Eunice's paper was published in the *AJSA* in 1856. At the time, Tyndall was working for the Royal Institution of Great Britain, a highly regarded scientific organization that subscribed to the *AJSA*. Tyndall was also on the editorial board of the *Philosophical Magazine,* a major scientific journal in England that also subscribed to the *AJSA*. That Tyndall would have had access to Eunice's paper doesn't prove that he read it, but Tyndall himself published a paper in the same 1856 edition of the *AJSA* in which Eunice's paper appeared. It was on the topic of "colour blindness." In the table of contents, the title of Tyndall's paper appears on page iv; Eunice's is on page vi. If Tyndall had read only the table of contents, he would have seen Eunice's title, "Circumstances Affecting the Heat of the Sun's Rays," three years before he conducted his experiment on the very same topic.

Moreover, in 1857, the *Philosophical Magazine* republished a paper of Elisha's that had been published in the same 1856 volume of the *AJSA* in which Eunice's and Tyndall's papers had appeared. It was titled "On the Heat in the Sun's Rays," a topic similar to Eunice's, though it had nothing to do with atmospheric gases and was not nearly as important as Eunice's work. Elisha's paper in the *AJSA* ran from pages 372 to 381; Eunice's started on page 382. In the mid-1800s, editorial board members of the *Philosophical Magazine* would have performed the peer review process themselves, rather than sending articles to outside reviewers. They could not possibly have read Elisha's paper without noticing Eunice's on the same topic in the same journal, printed right next to Elisha's.

Tyndall also would have learned about Eunice's work when, in 1857, the *Philosophical Magazine* republished Eunice's second scientific paper on static electricity, which had originally been published in the *AJSA*. Before making the decision to republish, editors would have asked whether Eunice had previously published any other scientific papers and quickly learned about her one and only other paper on the greenhouse effect from 1856.

Most importantly, when Tyndall said in 1859 that he was the first to discover the thermal effect of the sun's rays on carbon dioxide, he was declaring to the scientific community that he had checked all relevant journals to confirm that no paper on the same topic had previously been published. This was either an intentional lie meant to hide the truth, or he was supremely bad at research, because there were only about a thousand scientific journals worldwide in the mid-1800s (there are more than a hundred thousand today), and the *AJSA* was among the most prestigious. If he had checked only the most reputable publications, he would have learned of Eunice's paper.

Why Tyndall took credit for Eunice's work is unclear, but he was notorious for his sexism. He opposed voting rights for women and believed women were less intelligent than men. He said that women could read and understand science but not conceive new scientific ideas on their own.

About ten years after Tyndall's paper was published, Elizabeth Cady Stanton and Susan B. Anthony started a women's rights newspaper called *The Revolution*. They went to Washington, DC, to interview Eunice and Elisha for a story they were writing about women inventors and the patent process. By that time, Eunice had stopped doing experiments, and Elisha was head of the US Patent Office. The article in *The Revolution* included a quote from Eunice about why so few women were patent holders: "No doubt half the patents were the inventions of women but as men had the money to get up the models and loved notoriety, they had taken out all [the women's] names." It was also the case that married women often patented their inventions in the names of their husbands because they knew they had no rights of their own.

Eunice never found out that Tyndall had taken credit for her discovery. In fact, nobody noticed Tyndall's fraud until

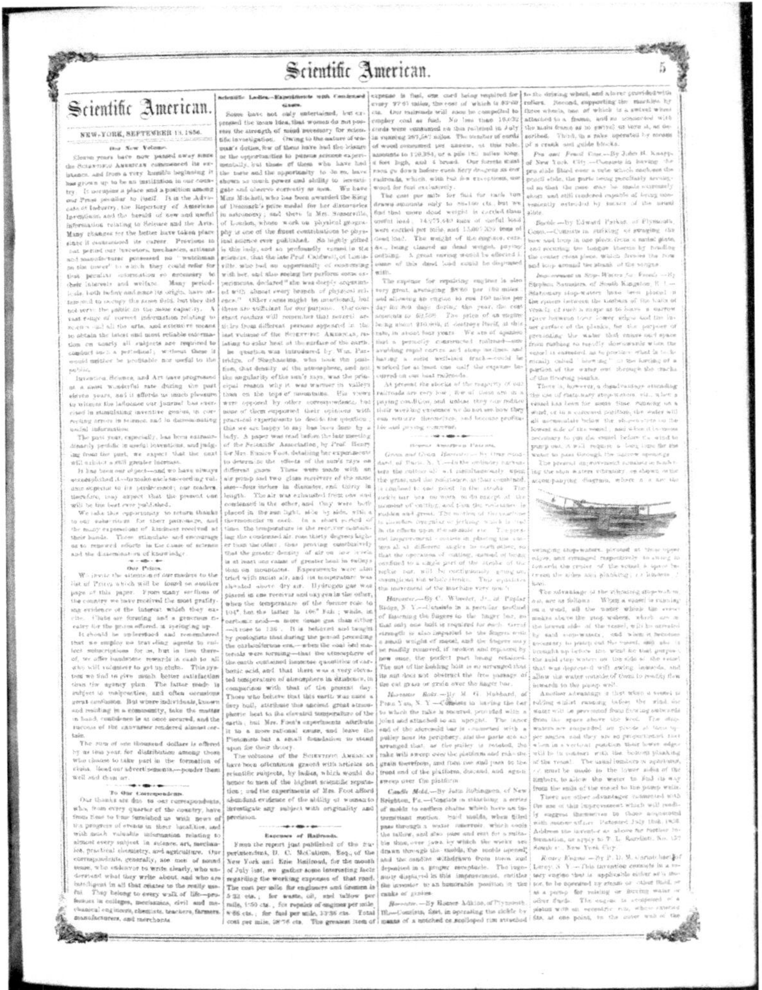

Scientific American. 5

Scientific American.

NEW-YORK, SEPTEMBER 13, 1856.

Scientific Ladies.—Experiments with Condensed Gases.

"Scientific Ladies—Experiments with Condensed Gases," describing Eunice's experiment in detail. From *Scientific American* 12, no. 1 (1856).

a retired geologist named Ray Sorenson, in 2010, happened across an article in the 1857 edition of the *Annual of Scientific Discovery* summarizing Eunice's experiment. Sorenson wrote a piece about Eunice's work in 2011 but declined to say whether he thought Tyndall had wrongly taken credit, because he could not determine whether Eunice had published her findings in a scientific journal.

A science historian named John Perlin was completing a book on solar energy when he read Sorenson's piece. Intrigued, he embarked on a years-long research project to determine whether Eunice had published her findings in 1856 and whether Tyndall knew about her work when he started conducting experiments on the same topic three years later. Perlin concluded that Tyndall had to have known. He shared his results at a 2019 exhibition at the University of California, Santa Barbara.

Perhaps as an act of karma, Tyndall's life did not end well. In 1893 his wife accidentally (we assume) gave him a fatal dose of chloral hydrate, which he had been taking for insomnia. One can only hope that he had trouble sleeping because he was racked with guilt about taking credit for Eunice's work.

Despite Tyndall's duplicity, he is widely known as the founder of climate science. Research institutes and even craters on the moon have been named for him because of his reputation as the man who discovered the greenhouse effect. Eunice enjoys no similar honors, though things are getting better. In 2022 the American Geophysical Union established the Eunice Newton Foote Medal for Earth-Life Science. And in 2023 the game show *Jeopardy* named Eunice as the person who discovered the greenhouse effect. Now we need a new *Jeopardy* category called "Men Who Steal," with a clue that goes something like this: "This woman-hating man took credit for Eunice Foote's discovery of global warming."

Learn More

Mandel, Kyla. "This Woman Fundamentally Changed Climate Science—and You've Probably Never Heard of Her." *Think Progress,* May 18, 2018. https://archive.thinkprogress.org/female-climate-scientist-eunice-foote-finally-honored-for-her-contributions-162-years-later-21b3cf08c70b/.

Ortiz, Joseph D., and Roland Jackson. "Understanding Eunice Foote's 1856 Experiments: Heat Absorption by Atmospheric Gases." *Notes and Records* 76 (2022): 67–84. https://doi.org/10.1098/rsnr.2020.0031.

2

A WOMAN DISCOVERED NUCLEAR FISSION; A MAN GOT HER PRIZE

Nuclear power is as fascinating as it is terrifying. Available in endless supply as a source of energy, it also threatens civilization as a weapon of mass destruction.

Nuclear power comes from a process known as fission. It's complicated, but essentially it means that the nucleus of an atom in a heavy chemical element, such as uranium or plutonium, when split by a neutron particle, converts mass into energy. The splitting makes the nucleus unstable, which causes it to produce new nuclei and new neutrons. The new neutrons then split the new nuclei, which produce more nuclei and more neutrons that then split the new nuclei, and so on. This chain reaction is why nuclear bombs cause such massive explosions.

The discovery of nuclear fission in the early 1900s was among the most important scientific achievements in history, and deservedly won a Nobel Prize, but a man named Otto Hahn got the award, instead of the woman who for decades had not only designed and conducted the experiments that led to Hahn's discovery but also explained nuclear fission to Hahn when he failed to comprehend it. That woman, Lise Meitner, deserved the Nobel Prize at least as much as Hahn did, but she wasn't even nominated.

Lise Meitner, 1953. Photograph by Robert R. Davis, courtesy of AIP Emilio Segrè Visual Archives, Physics Today Collection.

Lise Meitner was born in Vienna, Austria, on November 7, 1878, to Philipp and Hedwig Meitner. The third of eight children, Lise and her sisters were educated privately because women weren't allowed to attend public universities in Austria until 1897. Lise finished the equivalent of high school in 1892, at age fourteen, and finished eight years of college in only two. Lise was drawn to math and science, though she also became trained as a French teacher, because teaching was the only career offered to women at the time.

Lise entered a PhD program at the University of Vienna and graduated summa cum laude in 1906 with a degree in physics, the second woman to do so. She did research in optics, a new subcategory of physics, under the guidance of well-known theoretical physicists Paul Ehrenfest and Ludwig Boltzmann and was introduced to radioactivity, another new field, by experimental physicist Stefan Meyer. In 1907 Lise published a paper on alpha particles and atomic mass but, as a woman, had no prospects for a career in science, so she went to the Friedrich Wilhelm University (FWU; now Humboldt University of Berlin) to continue doing research as a postdoctoral student.

Although FWU was technically closed to women, Lise was so highly regarded that she was allowed to study there under the direction of renowned theoretical physicist and Nobel Prize winner Max Planck. She was also introduced to an Austrian chemist named Otto Hahn, who was Lise's age and was working on radioactivity. Lise was the only female scientist in the chemistry department and was forbidden to enter Hahn's lab, so she worked in the basement, where there were no bathrooms for women; she used a restroom at a nearby restaurant.

Lise worked with Hahn for more than three decades, from 1907 to 1938, though in 1912 they moved their research from FWU to the newly created Kaiser Wilhelm Institutes (KWI), also in Berlin. KWI was not a school—it focused on nuclear research and weapons development, not unlike the later-established Manhattan Project in the United States.

Lise's work was so impressive that the chemistry department at KWI was named the Hahn–Meitner Laboratory. Lise's status was equal to Hahn's, though she was paid less. Their lab focused on radioactive decay, and they made many important discoveries, but Lise did not receive equal credit. When Hahn was paid sixty-six thousand marks as royalties from their joint discovery of the radioactive isotope mesothorium, Lise got 10 percent. Only when Lise was offered a more lucrative academic position in Prague was her salary at KWI doubled to three thousand marks.

In 1922 Lise finally received an academic appointment; it was in the physics department at the University of Berlin. She was forty-four and had published more than forty scientific papers but was hired only as an adjunct lecturer. She taught there while also working at KWI and eventually became a full professor of physics—the first woman to achieve this status in all of Germany.

In 1929 a young chemist named Fritz Strassmann came to KWI. When his scholarship expired in 1932, Lise and Hahn hired him as their assistant. Two years later, Lise persuaded Hahn and Strassmann to focus on the work of Italian physicist Enrico Fermi, who was studying uranium. Fermi's research suggested that uranium could decay and produce new chemical elements, a process described at the time as transmutation. Over the next four years, Lise, Strassmann, and Hahn conducted several experiments on uranium using a technique called neutron bombardment, which involved using a neutron particle to "bombard" and split uranium atoms.

They initially thought neutron bombardment of uranium was creating new elements, as Fermi had described, but in 1937 Lise and Hahn published separate papers in different journals explaining how they disagreed about what they were actually seeing. Hahn's paper concluded—incorrectly, it would later turn out—that the production of new elements was consistent with existing knowledge of chemistry and needed no further investigation. Lise wasn't so sure. She wrote that it was unusual for neutron bombardment to cause uranium-238 to "capture" a neutron, produce triple isomers of uranium-239, and generate an unusually long sequence of beta decays. Lise said that what they were seeing could not be reconciled with "current ideas of nuclear structure" and needed more research. She designed new studies and continued directing Hahn and Strassmann in their work so they could better understand what they were witnessing with uranium.

Meanwhile, the Nazi regime had passed a law requiring the removal of Jews from civil service, including academia. As an Austrian Jew, Lise was initially exempted, but her status at KWI was not secure. In 1938, after Germany annexed Austria during the Anschluss, she lost her Austrian citizenship and was forced to flee Germany. Lise's uranium studies would have to be completed in her absence.

A Dutch physicist named Dirk Coster, whom Lise had met years earlier in Sweden, traveled to Germany to help her escape safely over the border to the Netherlands. Hahn gave her a diamond ring, reportedly to bribe officials if necessary, and at age fifty-nine, Lise left Germany by train and crossed the border into Holland on July 13, 1938. She then moved to Stockholm, Sweden, and took a position at the Nobel Institute for Physics.

In November 1938 Lise traveled to the Niels Bohr Institute in Copenhagen for a meeting with several scientists, including Hahn. Hahn and Strassmann had completed Lise's experiments and found what they believed was radium as a by-product of uranium. Lise was skeptical that they were seeing radium. She told Hahn to conduct further control studies to see if they could replicate the results, and that's exactly what Hahn did, because he and Strassmann always relied on Lise to guide them. As Strassmann would later say, her "opinion and judgement carried so much weight with us in Berlin that we immediately undertook the necessary control experiments."[1]

Hahn and Strassmann completed the additional research and discovered that Lise was correct. Neutron bombardment of uranium produced not radium but barium—something thought to be impossible because of barium's atomic size. Hahn was shocked. He wrote to Lise and described the results as "so peculiar" that he would not publish them unless she could come up with an explanation. He begged Lise for help because he could not make sense of the findings. His letter read, "We knew ourselves that it [uranium] can't actually burst apart into Ba [barium]. . . . So please think whether there is any possibility—perhaps a [barium] isotope with an atomic weight much higher than 137?" Hahn said that the idea that they were seeing barium was "physically absurd" and told Lise that she would "do a good deed" if she could explain their findings. Lise told Hahn that the results were "not impossible" or absurd and that she would send him an explanation.

Lise worked with her physicist nephew Otto Frisch to explain Hahn's results. Using Einstein's theory of relativity,

1. Ruth Lewin Sime, "Lise Meitner and the Discovery of Fission," *Journal of Chemical Education* 66, no. 5 (1989): 74.

Lise at Bryn Mawr College, April 1959. Courtesy of the Nuclear Regulatory Commission.

$E = mc^2$, they proved that it made scientific sense for uranium to produce barium.

Lise sent her explanation to Hahn, after which he and Strassmann quickly wrote a paper saying that their research proved that neutron bombardment of uranium produced barium. It was published in the German journal *Naturwissenschaften* on January 6, 1939, though it did not include an explanation of their results. On February 11, 1939, Lise coauthored an article with Frisch in the British journal *Nature,* describing mathematically why Hahn's findings made sense and why the process should be understood as nuclear fission. By the end of February, many scientists around the world had confirmed Lise's discovery of nuclear fission.

Though Hahn and Strassmann conducted many experiments as chemists, they depended on Lise's guidance because they were not as well trained in physics. As Lise famously told Hahn years earlier in Berlin, "Hahn, dear, of physics you understand nothing!" Lise, by contrast, was a theoretical and experimental physicist with a deep understanding of chemistry.

Despite Lise's significant role in the discovery of nuclear fission, she got no credit because she was forced to leave Germany before her experiments were completed. Strassmann thought this was unfair, saying, "What does it matter that Lise Meitner did not take direct part in the 'discovery'? . . . [She] has been the intellectual leader of our team." Hahn initially agreed, saying that the discovery of nuclear fission was the work of "three of us," but a few weeks after he published his landmark paper in January 1939, he began separating himself from Lise, saying that he and Strassmann "absolutely never did physics, but instead we did chemical separations over and over again. We know our limits and . . . in this case it was useful to do only chemistry. . . . For me the uranium work [discovery of fission] is a gift from heaven." Declaring the results "a gift from heaven" was Hahn's way of erasing Lise's paramount role in the discovery.

In 1944 the Nobel Prize was awarded to Hahn for *his* discovery of nuclear fission. By that time, he had achieved global fame for his January 1939 paper. Graciously responding to the slight by saying that Hahn deserved the prize, Lise also said that Hahn downplayed her significance and that without her guidance, he would never have studied the issue, much less discovered that splitting uranium produces nuclear energy. Lise was being modest, as it was she who designed and directed the countless uranium experiments on which she worked with Hahn over the years, and it was she who urged Hahn to conduct the control experiments that ended with his discovery of nuclear fission. Most important, it was Lise who explained to Hahn the significance and scientific logic of his findings when he failed to comprehend them on his own.

In response to critics who said Lise deserved the Nobel Prize, Hahn doubled down and issued a rude public statement saying that Lise was not involved in his discovery, though he apparently felt guilty because he gave Lise part of his cash award. Lise donated the money to Albert Einstein's Emergency Committee of Atomic Scientists, which promoted peaceful rather than military use of nuclear energy. She refused to work on any project related to the development of nuclear bombs and regretted that her work had led to their creation.

Lise talking to finalists in the Science Talent Search competition, Catholic University, spring 1946. *Left to right,* James Alexander Hummel, Lise Meitner, Iloka Karasz, James Benjamin Gibson, Stephen Reynolds Arnold, and George Loweree Gaines Jr. Courtesy the Smithsonian Institution.

During the course of her career, Lise received numerous prestigious awards and honors and was described by Albert Einstein as the "German Marie Curie." She was nominated for the Nobel Prize in Chemistry or in Physics forty-nine times. Hahn was nominated thirty-nine times, Strassmann only three times.

Thanks to science historians like Ruth Lewin Sime, PhD, Lise's story is becoming more widely known. Ruth wrote an article about Lise in 1989, explaining why she deserved credit for discovering nuclear fission. She then published a book about Lise's life in 1996. Ruth's dedication to the truth has helped inspire the scientific community to do more to recognize the significance of Lise's work. In 1997 the chemical element 109 was named "meitnerium" in Lise's honor. In

2010 the building where Lise did most of her research was renamed the Hahn–Meitner Building, after being known as the Otto Hahn Building for more than half a century. On November 6, 2020, a new satellite was named "Lise."

These honors are nice, but they pale in comparison to the value of a Nobel Prize. The Nobel Committee should give Lise a posthumous award, accompanied by a long overdue apology.

Learn More

Sime, Ruth Lewin. *Lise Meitner: A Life in Physics.* Berkeley: University of California Press, 1996.

3

HIDDEN NO MORE—BLACK WOMEN AT NASA

The highly acclaimed 2016 movie *Hidden Figures,* adapted from Margot Lee Shetterly's book of the same title, is a riveting story about three Black women who worked at NASA. Then known as NACA, the National Advisory Committee for Aeronautics, the organization employed the women as mathematicians, engineers, and computer scientists. The movie centers around the launch of Apollo 11, which sent astronauts to the moon in 1969. It was a historic event that had the whole world glued to the television, but the public didn't see the women behind the scenes whose work was instrumental to NASA's success. Only decades later would Margot and Hollywood step in to shine a light on the women's valuable contributions.

Dorothy Johnson Vaughan, Katherine Johnson, and Mary Winston Jackson were hired by NASA as "human computers" at a time when mechanical computers didn't exist or were inadequate. The women performed complex mathematical calculations that enabled NASA to control the speed and trajectory of rockets during a politically sensitive time when the United States was in a "Space War" with the Soviet Union.

Dorothy Johnson Vaughan, date unknown.

White women had been working for NASA as human computers since 1935, but Black women were not hired until after 1941, when President Roosevelt issued executive orders prohibiting race discrimination "in defense industries or government" and among "federal agencies" and "defense contractors." NASA took advantage of Roosevelt's orders and actively began recruiting Black female mathematicians in 1943. Despite the executive order's prohibition against race discrimination, Black women worked separately from white women and ate at separate tables.

Dorothy Johnson Vaughan was one of the first Black women hired to work at NASA. After her birth in Kansas City, Missouri, on September 20, 1910, Dorothy's family moved to Morgantown, West Virginia, where Dorothy graduated from Beechurst High School as class valedictorian in 1925. She went to college at Wilberforce University in Ohio and received a bachelor's degree in mathematics in 1929. She was encouraged to attend graduate school but instead took a job teaching math at a segregated high school in Farmville, Virginia, so she could help her family during the Great Depression.

Dorothy was married in 1932 and became a homemaker and mother to six children. She continued teaching until 1943, when NASA hired her to perform computations related to aircraft in wind tunnels. Her work helped NASA develop rockets with maximum efficiency by calculating how to minimize drag and increase lift. Put another way, Dorothy figured out, mathematically, how to make NASA's rockets fly as far and as fast as possible. In 1949 she became the first Black supervisor at NASA. The title allowed her to collaborate with male mathematicians and engineers on a variety of projects.

In 1958 NASA abolished its racially segregated working environment. This enabled Dorothy to join the newly established Analysis and Computation Division, which was developing NASA's first electronic computing department. Dorothy taught herself how to program computers, then taught computer programming to women colleagues so they could transition from human computing to programming jobs.

As a programmer, Dorothy helped develop a groundbreaking computer system that launched a 385-pound satellite into a five-hundred-mile orbit for the first time. She also worked on computations that ensured the success of America's first manned orbit around Earth, piloted by astronaut John Glenn in 1962.

Dorothy endured race and sex discrimination throughout her career, which inspired her to advocate for other women at NASA when they sought raises and better working conditions. Dorothy retired from NASA in 1971 and died on November 10, 2008.

Katherine Johnson, 1983. Courtesy NASA.

Katherine Johnson was hired by NASA nearly ten years after Dorothy Vaughan. Born in White Sulphur Springs, West Virginia, on August 26, 1918, as Creola Katherine Coleman, Katherine was a very bright child. She was drawn to math and completed the eighth grade at age ten. Because there were no schools in her area where Black people could achieve education beyond eighth grade, her family moved 120 miles away to Institute, West Virginia, where Katherine attended high school.

After graduating at age fourteen, Katherine enrolled at West Virginia State College, where she studied under Dr. William W. Schieffelin Claytor, the third Black person to earn a PhD in mathematics. Katherine graduated summa cum laude in 1937 at age eighteen with dual degrees in mathematics and French. She taught for a while at a segregated public school in Virginia before marrying James Goble and resigning from teaching in 1939. She then entered a master's degree program in mathematics but left graduate school to start a family, eventually giving birth to six children. In 1952 she was hired by NASA.

Katherine was unusually assertive and curious, and her work was superior to others', so she was promoted to the Flight Research Division after only two weeks. NASA was having trouble figuring out how to guarantee that a space capsule would land at a certain location upon its return to Earth. Katherine was confident she could do the calculations and said, "You tell me when you want it and where you want it to land, and I'll do [the calculations] backwards and tell you when to take off."[1] Katherine's mathematical formula enabled NASA to send a human being into space for the first time. Alan Shepard was launched into space in 1961 and returned safely to Earth fifteen minutes later.

NASA next wanted to send a man into orbit around Earth, which required more complicated calculations because of gravitational pull. By this time, NASA was using computers, but their computations were not always correct. Katherine was assigned to validate the work of the machines, which led to John Glenn's successful orbit in 1962.

Katherine also performed vital calculations for NASA's historic Apollo 11 launch in 1969, when Neil Armstrong walked on the moon and uttered his famous line, "That's one small step for man, one giant leap for mankind." And in 1970, when Apollo 13 experienced a computer malfunction in

1. NASA History, "Mathematician Katherine Johnson at Work," February 25, 2016, https://www.nasa.gov/image-feature/mathematician-katherine-johnson-at-work.

space, it was Katherine who did the calculations that brought the astronauts safely back to Earth.

Katherine retired from NASA in 1971 and passed away on February 24, 2020, at age 101.

Mary Winston Jackson was hired by NASA as a human computer in 1951, a year before Katherine Johnson. Mary was born in Hampton, Virginia, on April 9, 1921, and graduated from high school with the highest honors in 1937. She then studied at the Hampton Institute and earned dual degrees in mathematics and physical science in 1942. Like Katherine and Dorothy, Mary's first job out of college was as a teacher in a segregated school, but a year later, she began working as a bookkeeper close to home. In 1944 she married Levi Jackson and started a family, eventually giving birth to two children.

In 1951 Mary took a job at the Office of the Chief Army Field Forces at Fort Monroe in Virginia and from there was recruited by NASA to work as a human computer under Dorothy's supervision. In 1953, after lodging a complaint about racially segregated working conditions, Mary was moved to NASA's Compressibility Research Division, which was integrated. She worked directly with an engineer named Kazimierz Czarnecki, who encouraged her to become trained as an engineer. To do that, she needed to take graduate-level math classes, which were offered in the evening, but only at an all-white school. Mary went to court and won the right to take the classes. She completed the program in 1958 and was promoted to aerospace engineer. She was the first Black female engineer at NASA.

Mary eventually became an expert analyst in several NASA divisions and authored twelve research and technical papers. Her work contributed significantly to NASA's many successes in its space program.

In 1979 Mary left her job as an engineer and became the manager of Langley's Federal Women's Program, which was basically NASA's antidiscrimination and affirmative action office. Mary dedicated the rest of her career at NASA to helping women and racial minorities achieve equality in employment. She passed away in 2005 at age eighty-three.

Mary Winston Jackson working at NASA, 1977. Courtesy NASA.

Thanks to Hollywood, Dorothy, Katherine, and Mary are finally getting the credit they deserve, but their stories might never have been told if it hadn't been for the curiosity and hard work of a woman named Margot Lee Shetterly. Margot was visiting her parents for Christmas in 2010 when her father, a retired NASA engineer, began talking about some of the Black women he knew who had worked at NASA as human computers. Margot was intrigued and decided to write a book. Before it was even finished, Hollywood bought the rights and started making a movie.

As a child, Margot knew that Black women worked at NASA because she sometimes went to the office with her father and saw them there, but she did not understand their significance until she began doing research. The more she learned, the more compelled she felt to tell their stories. As a Black woman, Margot knew firsthand what it felt like to be disrespected. She often tells the story of how, as a little girl, she was insatiably curious and, at the tender age of eight, went to the library to check out a stack of books about the stock market. The librarian looked at Margot, then looked at the subject matter of the books, and told her she should not be a gopher who goes to the library to take out books for other people. It was the first time Margot experienced someone making an unfair assumption about her abilities.

Margot's accidental discovery of inspiring stories about Black women at NASA begs us to find more "hidden figures." Every time one woman's story is told, there's a chance it could lead to other untold stories. Here's a good example: we all know about Rosa Parks, the woman who bravely refused to obey a local ordinance in Montgomery, Alabama, that required Black people to sit in the back of public buses, but if Rosa's story hadn't been told, we might never have learned about Claudette Colvin, who did the same thing on the same bus system nine months earlier, when she was only fifteen years old. Initially obedient, Claudette was sitting in the back of the bus when a white woman boarded and found no available seats in the white section. She asked Claudette and her friends to move farther back so she could sit in one of their seats. Her friends moved, but Claudette refused. The white woman declined to sit in one of the seats left open by Claudette's friends because Black people were not allowed to sit next to white people. Police were called, and Claudette was told to move, but she insisted that she had a right to stay where she was. Police physically removed her, handcuffed her, and took her to jail. A judge later dropped the charges to prevent Claudette from appealing and overturning the law, but she then became one of several plaintiffs in a 1956 lawsuit that struck down the segregated bus ordinance as unconstitutional.

Rosa led us to Claudette, just like the women in *Hidden Figures* led us to these other Black women who did important work at NASA:

» Miriam Daniel Mann worked at NASA from 1943 to 1966, after graduating from Talladega College with a chemistry degree and a minor in mathematics. Like the women in *Hidden Figures,* Miriam was hired as a human computer to solve complex math problems. She worked directly on the mission that put the first man into space, and although she died two years before Neil Armstrong walked on the moon, her work directly supported that mission. Miriam spoke up against racism and segregation at NASA, once removing a sign that directed "colored" people to sit at a certain table in the back of the cafeteria.

» Kathryn Peddrew worked at NASA as a human computer in 1943, though that was not the job for which she had applied. She had a degree in chemistry, so she was hired as a chemist. But when NASA learned she was Black, they transferred her to the human computer division. Like Miriam and the others, Kathryn worked on complex math problems related to space launches and contributed to NASA's success.

» Christine Darden went to NASA in the late 1960s, decades after Miriam and Kathryn, though not much had changed. She had a master's degree in engineering but was sent, like the others, to work as a human computer. Her skills as an engineer were beneficial to NASA, but NASA could pay her less if she worked in the human computer department. Eventually Christine complained and was transferred to an engineering position in 1973, where she did research and solved math problems related to the science behind sonic boom, the thunder-like noise created by shock waves when an object travels through the air faster than the speed of sound. Christine published more than fifty scholarly papers on the topic and earned her PhD in 1983.

» Annie Eastley was hired at NASA in 1955, and she, too, was sent to work in the human computer division. Annie was eventually trained to write computer code and worked on the design of an important new computer program known as Centaur. Centaur was critical to the success of more than 220 space launches and is still being used today as the foundation for other codes used in military, weather, and communication satellites. When Annie started working at NASA, NASA had a policy of paying tuition costs when employees took

> college classes relevant to their work, so she asked NASA to pay for math classes at a local community college. NASA declined, saying it paid only for "professionals" to take courses, and people who worked in the human computer division were considered subprofessional. Annie paid for her own classes and earned a bachelor's degree in mathematics.

Hidden Figures brought us stories of amazing women, but more importantly, it inspired us to wonder about all the other "hidden" women out there who deserve to have their stories told.

Learn More

Shetterly, Margot Lee. *Hidden Figures: The American Dream and the Untold Story of the Black Women Mathematicians Who Helped Win the Space Race.* New York: William Morrow Paperbacks, 2016.

4

HE SAID HER PAINTINGS WERE HIS—AND TOOK ALL THE MONEY

If you've ever served as a juror, you know that real trials are nothing like what you see on television—there are no *Perry Mason* moments when a witness bursts into tears and confesses to being the real killer. But Margaret Keane's very real lawsuit against her ex-husband for claiming that he was the artist behind her famous paintings gave us one of the most dramatic courtroom moments in history.

Margaret was born in Nashville, Tennessee, on September 15, 1927, to David and Jessie Hawkins. She suffered a severe injury to her eardrum when she was a toddler, which left her with hearing loss. Margaret learned to focus on people's eyes to better understand what they were saying. At age ten, she started drawing and took art classes at the Watkins Institute, an art and design college in Nashville. At eighteen, she moved to New York City and attended the Traphagen School of Design. A year later, she started her career as an artist, painting clothing and furniture.

In 1948 Margaret married Frank Ulbrich, and the couple had a daughter. Margaret shifted the focus of her art to portrait painting, mostly of women, children, and animals.

In 1955 Margaret divorced Ulbrich and moved with her

daughter to San Francisco, California, where she met her second husband, Walter Keane, at an outdoor art exhibition. He was a charismatic and handsome man who would later claim that when Margaret met him, she saw his paintings of big-eyed children and told him he was the "greatest artist" she had ever seen. In fact, Walter was not much of an artist at all.

After a whirlwind romance, the couple married in 1955 in Hawai'i. They settled in San Francisco, where Margaret began painting mostly imaginary people, often children with unusually large eyes. She called them "Big Eyes" and said they were "an expression of her own deepest feelings." Margaret could paint almost anything, but she preferred making Big Eyes because "eyes are windows to the soul."

Margaret signed her Big Eyes paintings with the name "Keane" and displayed them at the hungry i nightclub in San Francisco, famous for its hippie reputation and for launching Lenny Bruce as a comedian. They were also shown at galleries in New York, Chicago, and New Orleans. Margaret was shy and relied on Walter to sell her pieces because he was, according to her, a "master" at marketing and sales. In time the Big Eyes paintings became very popular and sold for as much as $50,000 each. Margaret was delighted, until she learned that Walter was telling buyers that he was the artist. When she complained, Walter urged Margaret to go along with the fraud because buyers would pay more if they thought he was the painter. He also said buyers would sue both of them if the truth came out, and he threatened to have Margaret and her daughter killed by the Mafia if she exposed him. Margaret was terrified. Walter was an abusive alcoholic who had kicked their pet chihuahua so often she gave the dog away to protect him. Margaret stayed silent while Walter became an international art sensation, even traveling to Tokyo in 1964 to be photographed with the director of the National Museum of Western Art when they acquired two of Margaret's paintings.

Margaret received no money for her paintings, though she and Walter moved into a nice home with a swimming pool. Margaret painted for sixteen hours a day, while Walter lived the high life, having parties and often inviting other women into their home for sexual liaisons.

A-2 The DAILY REPORT, Ontario-Upland, Calif., Thurs., Oct. 15, 1970

Who Painted Eyes?

Wife Challenges Artist's Acclaim

SAN FRANCISCO (UPI)— Margaret Keane McGuire wants to settle, once and for all, the true identity of artist responsible for the "eyes" of the internationally-known "Keane" paintings of children.

In a recent issue of Life magazine, Walter Keane likened himself to Rembrandt, El Greco, Michaelangelo and refused to concede that anyone of them could top him as a painter of eyes.

But Margart Keane McGuire, in San Francisco to complete work on a lithograph series, said Wednesday it was she who did all the "eyes" paintings and issued a direct challenge to her ex-husband.

"Give us both paint and brush and canvas and turn us loose in Union Square (in the heart of downtown San Francisco) at high noon and we'll see who can paint eyes," she said. "I'd like that."

She said her former husband had a genius for "marketing and publicity," but he had absolutely none for painting.

"I couldn't even teach him to paint," Mrs. McGuire said. "I did the paintings. Sometimes he painted a little of the backgrounds. He was the one who promoted the paintings and sold them. I can paint and he can't.

"I stayed home and painted and did the housework," said Mrs. Mcguire, now a resident of Honolulu, "and Walter sold them in the hungry i.

"He wanted to learn to paint and I tried to teach him to paint when he was home— which wasn't often. He couldn't even learn to paint."

She continued, "I signed the paintings 'Keane,' my married name. When I asked him why he said he was the painter, he said the buyers always wanted to pay more if they met the painter.

"After we started to make it, it didn't make any difference. All I got out of it was a larger house to keep. And I always did the faces and the eyes and he might touch up the background.

"I didn't know how to get out. I finally gave up and one day I just left and went to Honolulu."

Asked why she had remained silent about who painted the "eyes" for five years after the Keane divorce, she said:

"People keep asking me and I decided to tell the truth."

Keane was not available for comment.

The "eyes" are the hallmark and trademark of the art form that flourished into the international art trade market more than a decade ago.

Story from the *Daily Report* (Ontario-Upland, CA), October 15, 1970.

Margaret painted in an isolated room during the day, with curtains closed and the door shut. When Walter was out, he would call home to make sure she was still working. Margaret described her life as "jail." She painted all the time and gave Walter her pieces to sell. Walter would collect the money and tell Margaret what types of paintings to do next, demanding each day when he returned home, "What did you paint today?"

Margaret grew tired of Walter's abuse and divorced him in 1965. She then met and married a sportswriter from Hawai'i named Dan McGuire, who encouraged her to tell the public about Walter's fraud. Margaret went on a radio show in 1970 and revealed that she was the real artist behind the Big Eyes paintings. Walter was furious. He told the media he was "flabbergasted" that his shy ex-wife would lie. He claimed he was inspired to paint the Big Eyes portraits while living in war-torn Berlin in 1946. He said he would stare heartbroken at the faces of big-eyed, hungry children fighting for scraps of food and that he would sketch them as an act of "frantic despair."

With the help of news organizations, Margaret challenged Walter to a public paint-off to prove who was the real artist. It was scheduled to take place in San Francisco's Union Square in October 1970, but Walter never showed up. *LIFE* magazine was there because it had published a story attributing Margaret's work to Walter. After Margaret easily painted one of her signature portraits, the magazine published a story correcting its mistake.

Margaret and Dan eventually moved to Hawai'i, where, in 1986, Margaret filed a federal lawsuit against Walter and *USA Today* for falsely claiming that Walter was the Big Eyes painter. To determine who was telling the truth, the judge ordered Walter and Margaret to create a Big Eyes painting in front of the jury. Margaret completed her piece in an hour, while Walter refused to paint at all, claiming he had a sore shoulder. After a three-and-a-half-week trial, the jury awarded Margaret $4 million. Walter never paid Margaret a dime despite having earned millions from the sale of Margaret's work. Margaret didn't care. She was satisfied that the public now knew, unequivocally, that she was the Big Eyes painter.

After Dan died, Margaret returned to California to live with her daughter. Devoutly religious, Margaret continued to paint and enjoy success not only as the Big Eyes artist but also as a portrait painter. Celebrities such as Jerry Lewis, Joan Crawford, and Natalie Wood commissioned Margaret to paint them and their families. Walter lived a miserable and destitute life until his death in 2000.

Margaret's story became international news in 2014 when a Hollywood movie was made about her life. Directed by renowned filmmaker Tim Burton, *Big Eyes* starred Academy Award–winning actress Amy Adams as Margaret. Margaret said the film was difficult to watch because she had to relive the abuse she suffered during her marriage to Walter. She was especially shaken by the actor who played Walter, Christopher Waltz, because he looked, sounded, and behaved just like him. Still, Margaret thought the movie was "fantastic." There she was on the big screen—standing up against her monstrous ex-husband while he withered in shame. By then in her late eighties, the woman who once considered herself too timid to confront Walter smiled as the whole world watched her take him down.

Margaret died on June 26, 2022, at age ninety-four. Her Big Eyes paintings continue to sell well, and thanks to Hollywood, everyone knows the truth about who painted them.

Learn More

Keane Eyes Gallery, https://www.keane-eyes.com/. For the court exhibit painting, see https://www.keane-eyes.com/product/exhibit-224/.

5

A WOMAN INVENTED MONOPOLY TO DISCOURAGE GREED, THEN A GREEDY MAN STOLE IT

Who doesn't love Monopoly? Even with fast-paced video games at our fingertips, we still want the thrill of owning a hotel on Boardwalk and getting $200 in fake money just to pass Go. The game's objective is simple: Players buy properties so that other players have to pay them rent. They move around the board in the hope of not landing on someone else's property or going to jail. Whoever doesn't go bankrupt wins.

The game was originally invented to inspire people not to be greedy by helping them understand how sad it is when one person gets all the money and everyone else goes broke. That was the plan when a woman named Elizabeth Magie came up with the idea for the game in the late 1800s. But when a man stole her creation and claimed it as his own, it quickly became a game that celebrated greed. Ironically, the truth did not become widely known until the 1970s, when a lawsuit driven by greed revealed Elizabeth as the true inventor.

Elizabeth Magie was born to Mary Jane and James Magie in Macomb, Illinois, on May 9, 1866. James was a newspaper publisher and well-known abolitionist. The family moved to Maryland in the early 1880s, where Elizabeth worked

Elizabeth Magie, 1892.

variously as a writer, reporter, stenographer, actor, inventor, and engineer. She got her first patent at age twenty-six, for an invention that improved the functionality of typewriters.

Elizabeth was also a feminist. When she realized that women were not paid enough to support themselves and that this incentivized women to get married, she placed an advertisement in a local newspaper auctioning herself off as a "young woman American slave" who was looking for a husband to own her. Elizabeth wanted people to understand that women were not free and were controlled by the wealth and power of white men. The ad created a lot of controversy and established Elizabeth as a leader in the feminist community.

Elizabeth embraced progressive values and was influenced by the popular book *Progress and Poverty* by Henry George. The book was critical of laws and policies that created wide disparities in wealth and argued that a land tax rather than an income tax would best promote democracy by preventing landowners from acquiring disparate power and influence. Elizabeth believed that all people should be encouraged to cultivate land and own the value of their work. This philosophy inspired her to create a board game she called the Landlord's Game. She designed the rules to help people

SAYS GIRLS ARE SLAVES

Elizabeth Magie So Decides After Interviewing Maids of the Typewriter.

WORK HARD ALL DAY AND HAVE NO FREEDOM

Some Would Like to Travel, All Like to Read, but Not One Likes Her Vocation.

Special to Detroit Free Press.

Chicago, October 27.—Elizabeth Magie, Chicago's "white slave," has again come into the limelight. Chicago papers published a signed interview on "Why a ten-dollar a week typewriter girl is a white slave." In this she says: "'What would you rather do than typewriting?' I asked a $10 a week typewriter.

"'Oh, I don't know,' she said. Then she folded her hands, looked up at the rim of her big brown hat and answered:

"'Why, I would like to sing in the chorus. The girls say I have a lovely voice, and I love to sing.'

"'Why don't you go on the stage then? Can't you get as much as you get at ty ewriting?'

"'Oh, yes, more' but my parents educated me in stenography and typewriting, and I suppose I've got to do that; but I hate it. I would rather do housework. Why don't I get married? Because I don't know the right fellow. But I would rather marry anybody, most, than do typewriting.'

"This young lady probably would resent the idea of selling herself; nevertheless, should she enter into mariage merely to escape from typewriting it would be nothing more nor less than a sale.

"'What would I like to do most?' said another $10 a week stenographer, an intelligent, keen-witted girl, who looked as though she would make something worth while out of herself if she only had half a chance.

"'I would like to travel and see the world. If it wasn't for the thought of being a sort of servant I sometimes think I would like to be a lady's maid to some actress. I could get to see the world then. Besides, these maids always live well and dress well.'

"'You like nice clothes, then, do you?' I asked.

"'You bet I do. And they like you better and treat you better when you are well dressed, too.'

"Her definition of a 'slave' was 'one who has to work hard and who isn't free to come and go.'

"'Are you a slave?' I inquired.

"'N-no.'

"She didn't like to admit it.

"'You work hard all day, you say, for $10 a week, and you are not free to come and go, then, aren't you a slave?' I concluded.

"No answer.

"I talked with several other girls, particularly typewriters and stenographers asking them all particularly the same questions. In answer to the question, 'What do you read?' most of them replied that they read novels and magazine stories. One would like to be a traveler, liked books on travel; another [illegible] history and one read only newspapers. Only one said she would rather hear a sermon than see a play. As to the novel readers, one admitted frankly that she liked sensational love stories the best. Most of the others say they didn't like trashy novels, they liked stories with something in them.

"The young girls—most of them, don't want to read tracts on economic subjects; when they read they do so principally for amusement. Therefore I suggest stories that instruct as well as entertain."

MOTHERS O. K. SUNDAY FUN

IOWA WOMEN APPROVE OF BUSTER BROWN, ET AL.

Des Moines, October 27.—Happy Hooligan, "Buster Brown" and other denizens of the comic Sunday papers, found a champion in Miss Alice Hopper, one of the most noted kindergarten educators in the country, before the Iowa Congress of Mothers at the Unitarian church today. While a member was deploring the fascination which the funny papers have for their children on Sunday, Miss Hopper declared that she could see no harm in the Sunday "funny" papers and did not believe they had a bad effect on the children.

"I do not believe the funny papers have a pernicious influence on the children any more on Sunday than they would have on a week day," said Miss Hopper, "and, besides, men are only children grown up, and if the comics are not good for your children they are not good for your husbands."

The Mothers' Congress heartily indorsed Miss Hopper's remarks by resolution.

Elizabeth advertises herself as a slave in the *Detroit Free Press*, October 28, 1906.

understand why allowing a small number of people to accumulate land causes harm to the majority, who do not own land.

Elizabeth made her first version of the game by hand in 1897. It was a square board with spaces along the sides that represented properties players could purchase when they landed on them. Less expensive properties had names like Rickety Row, whereas more expensive properties were named Fifth Avenue and Wall Street. The middle space on each side was a railroad, and there were spaces for Chance, the Poor House, Go to Jail, and "necessities" like shelter, food, and clothing.

The game had two sets of rules. One was called the "single-tax variant," which required players to interact cooperatively with one another and learn how a public tax on land would benefit all players. The other was called the "monopoly variant," which incentivized players to accumulate property, acquire wealth, and drive other players into bankruptcy. Elizabeth wanted people to play both versions so they could understand the differences between the two systems and see how harmful it was to live under an economic system that encouraged greed.

Board games were popular at the turn of the century because the growing middle class was buying homes, working regular hours, and enjoying activities that brought the family together at the end of the workday. Elizabeth's Landlord's Game was so popular that others copied it and added variations to the rules. Elizabeth saw the growing value of her game and obtained a patent for it in 1904.

In 1924 Elizabeth got another patent for a revised version of her game. She gave the properties colors, organized them into groups of two and three, changed the rules a bit, and added spots for Lord Blueblood's Estate, Luxury Tax, and Income Tax. She tried unsuccessfully to sell her patent to toy companies.

A religious group known as the Quakers loved Elizabeth's game because they disavowed greed. They appreciated the lesson Elizabeth was trying to teach but wanted to call the game Monopoly. They made their own version and changed the property names to actual street names in Atlantic City,

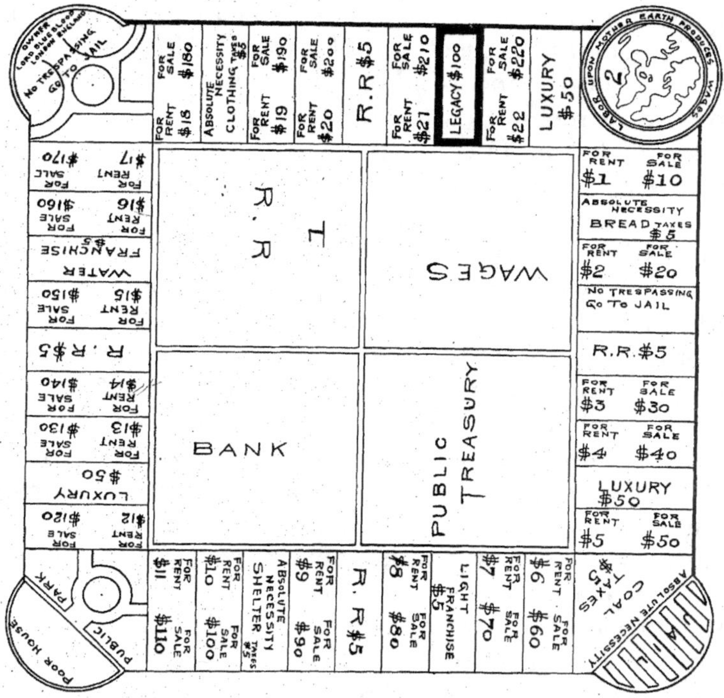

Elizabeth's original game board design. Courtesy US National Archives.

New Jersey. The least expensive properties were named for streets where the poorest people lived, while the more expensive properties, such as Park Place and Boardwalk, were named for waterfront streets where the wealthiest people lived and where the casinos were located. The Quakers did not try to patent or profit from their game—they played it with friends and family and used it to inspire generosity and kindness.

In 1934 a Quaker woman named Esther Jones had a dinner party where one of the guests was a man she knew from Quaker school named Charles Todd. Todd brought Monopoly to the party, and they played after dinner. Esther's husband, Charles Darrow, liked the game so much that he asked Todd for a copy of the rules. Unemployed at the time, Darrow made his own version of the game by changing the artwork a bit, though he copied most of it from Todd's version. He even copied the incorrect spelling the Quakers had used for a real street in New Jersey, Marven Gardens, which was misspelled "Marvin Gardens."

Like Elizbeth, Darrow tried to sell his stolen version to toy companies, but they weren't interested, so he manufactured it himself and got it on store shelves for the 1934 Christmas season. It sold so well that Parker Brothers offered to buy it from him in 1935 for $7,000 plus future royalties. Parker Brothers then helped Darrow patent the game, and before long, Monopoly was sweeping the nation. In 1936 Parker Brothers sold thirty-five thousand games *per week*.

Parker Brothers soon became suspicious of Darrow's claim that he was the original creator. When the company confronted him, he insisted that he was the inventor, though he could not explain how he came up with the idea for the game. When asked how he knew the names of streets in Atlantic City, Darrow said he had gone there as a child for vacation. Parker Brothers didn't believe him. The company renegotiated his contract to protect itself from legal trouble, then started promoting his claims about inventing Monopoly in its advertising campaigns. It even included a heartwarming story about Darrow inside the game box—it said he "invented" Monopoly during the Great Depression to amuse himself because he was unemployed.

Parker Brothers later learned that numerous other versions of the game existed, so it started buying the rights to all of them. Most were not patented, but Elizabeth's was, so Parker Brothers offered her a few hundred dollars and promised to mass-produce her Landlord's Game and give her royalties on sales. Elizabeth was delighted. Parker Brothers began manufacturing the Landlord's Game, but a year later, it took the game off the market.

Elizabeth was not happy that Darrow was getting credit for her invention. She told the media about how she invented Monopoly and that Darrow had stolen her idea and claimed it as his own. Darrow denied Elizabeth's claims and said the idea for Monopoly came to him like a "freak of nature."

Parker Brothers needed to silence Elizabeth, so it gave her more money for two other games she had created, but they did not sell. Elizabeth's story faded as Darrow became a millionaire and gained global fame as the man who invented Monopoly.

Elizabeth died in 1948 with hardly anyone knowing that she had invented Monopoly, but in 1973 the truth started to come out when Parker Brothers filed a copyright infringement lawsuit against a college professor named Ralph Anspach, who had invented a game called Anti-Monopoly as a protest against the Parker Brothers game. To win, Parker Brothers had to prove that Darrow was the inventor. For Anspach to win, he had to prove that Elizabeth was the inventor. After a ten-year legal battle that went all the way to the US Supreme Court, Anspach won; he was free to continue selling his Anti-Monopoly game, and Parker Brothers had to stop saying that Monopoly was Darrow's invention. The story inside the box was changed from Darrow "invented" Monopoly to Darrow "presented" Monopoly to Parker Brothers. Eventually, Darrow's lie was removed altogether, and today's version makes no mention of the impostor.

It was a fitting end to Elizbeth's story. The company that bastardized a game she invented to teach people that greed is bad lost millions because of its own greed. Better yet, the lawsuit Parker Brothers hoped would erase Elizabeth Magie once and for all instead shined a bright light on the truth and established Elizabeth forevermore as Monopoly's true creator.

Learn More

Pilon, Mary. *The Monopolists: Obsession, Fury, and the Scandal behind the World's Favorite Board Game.* New York: Bloomsbury, 2016.

6

SHE MIGHT HAVE BECOME LEGENDARY, BUT HER PAINTINGS DEPICTED WOMEN AS MEN'S EQUALS

In 1971, feminist art historian Linda Nochlin published an essay titled "Why Have There Been No Great Women Artists?" Her answer: there were many, but the men who wrote the history books didn't include them.

Among the women about whom Nochlin wrote was a celebrated baroque painter of the seventeenth century named Artemisia Gentileschi. Nochlin said she was excluded because art is a patriarchal institution and the men in charge did not want women to enjoy the influence or financial rewards art had to offer. Others argue that Artemisia was erased from history to punish her for accusing a powerful man of rape and for daring to depict women as men's equals in her paintings. In addition to Artemisia being ignored, several of her paintings were wrongfully attributed to men.

Born in Rome in 1593, Artemisia learned to paint from her father, Orazio, after her mother died in childbirth when Artemisia was twelve. Orazio was a well-known artist whose paintings reflected those of his friend, famed Roman painter Caravaggio (Michelangelo Merisi). Caravaggio developed the baroque style of painting, which is grand

Artemisia Gentileschi, *Susanna and the Elders,* 1610. Oil on canvas, 67 × 47 in. Schloss Weißenstein, Pommersfelden, Germany.

and shows movement. Baroque paintings usually depict people expressing intense emotion, and objects are often allegorical, for example, a skeleton may be used to symbolize death.

Artemisia enjoyed painting biblical stories, which was unusual for female artists of the time, who typically painted only still lifes, portraits, and family scenes. Although Artemisia learned from her father, she developed her own technique and painted people in their natural state, while her father idealized the subjects of his work.

Artemisia's earliest known piece is a 1610 painting titled *Susanna and the Elders*. Completed when Artemisia was only

Jan Massys, *Susanna and the Elders,* 1564. Oil on panel, 51 3/4 × 43 7/8 in. Compare the treatment of the subjects to those in Artemisia's painting. Private collection.

sixteen, it depicts the biblical story of a young woman named Susanna being accosted by two men begging her for sex and threatening to ruin her reputation if she rejects them. Male artists who painted the same story often portrayed the men as cheerful and harmless, while Susanna appears unaffected or even flattered by the attention. Artemisia, by contrast, painted Susanna as disgusted, with her face painfully turned away from the men, who seem conspiratorial and lecherous. Art scholars today see the piece as reflecting Artemisia's personal experiences of men harassing her, including her father's friend and fellow artist Agostino Tassi.

Tassi was more than twice Artemisia's age, but he was obsessed with her. On a day in 1611 when Orazio was not home, Tassi saw Artemisia painting in her father's studio and admonished her not to "paint so much." He threw her paintbrushes and palette and forced Artemisia into a nearby bedroom. Tassi locked the door, pushed her onto a bed, and held her down by her breasts. He forced his knee between her legs, covered her mouth with a handkerchief, and raped her. Artemisia scratched Tassi's face, pulled his hair, and grabbed his penis so roughly she tore off a piece of skin, but he did not stop. After the rape, Artemisia took a knife from a dresser drawer and threatened to kill him. Tassi opened his coat and mockingly said, "Here I am." Artemisia threw the knife but didn't hurt him.

When Artemisia told her father what had happened, Orazio insisted that Tassi marry her and restore the family's reputation. Tassi initially agreed but changed his mind, so Orazio filed a criminal rape charge against him. In the 1600s rape was not a crime against a woman; it was a theft of the family's honor. Tassi had devalued the family by taking Artemisia's virginity, so it was Orazio who had the right to file a complaint. Charges would have been impossible if Artemisia had not been a virgin.

Soon after the rape, Artemisia painted her most famous piece, *Judith Slaying Holofernes* (1612–13). It depicts the biblical story of Judith beheading an enemy of the Israelites. In Artemisia's interpretation, Holofernes lies face up on a bed, his head hanging over the edge, while Judith grips

Artemisia Gentileschi, *Judith Slaying Holofernes,* 1612–13. Oil on canvas, 78 1/3 × 64 1/8 in. Museo Capodimonte, Naples, Italy.

his hair with one hand to hold his head steady while slicing through his neck with a large sword. Judith's maid Abra is also in the scene—she holds Holofernes down by his chest as his oversized, outstretched fist nearly reaches her face. The painting is notable for its grisly details, spurting blood, and expressions on the faces of the two women, who seem determined, nonplussed, and confident. Holofernes's eyes, by contrast, are open and filled with terror as he realizes he is about to die. Many scholars describe the piece as a "revenge painting," where Artemisia is showing herself as Judith exacting revenge against Tassi for raping her. Others see an even more profound message about women working together, across class lines, against their common enemy: abusive men. In the biblical story, Abra is standing in a nearby room during the beheading while Judith alone kills Holofernes, and many male artists who have painted the scene depict Abra standing a distance away. Artemisia's interpretation has Abra and Judith working in solidarity to overpower and kill Holofernes. Years later, Artemisia painted a new version of the piece in which she added a bracelet to Judith's left arm, decorated with images of Artemis, Greek goddess of the hunt and Artemisia's namesake.

Tassi's rape trial began in 1612 and went on for months. Tassi denied raping Artemisia, but his credibility was ruined when evidence came out that he had previously raped his sister-in-law, was suspected of having had his missing wife murdered, and had plans to steal Orazio's art. Artemisia's credibility was assessed differently. She was forced to submit to a vaginal exam so the court could determine whether she was a virgin. Seemingly barbaric by today's standards, such exams are still conducted on rape victims in some states. In 2009 a West Virginia judge named David Wright ordered a child rape victim to submit to a forced vaginal exam so her hymen could be examined by an expert witness for the defense. The highest court in West Virginia upheld the order, ruling idiotically that the government forcing a rape victim to undergo an unwanted, penetrating vaginal exam at the behest of her attacker is no different than a visit to a gynecologist.

After the vaginal exam, Artemisia's credibility was subjected to a form of torture known as the *sibille*. Court officials wrapped her fingers in rope and twisted tighter and tighter to see whether she would change her story when the pain became unbearable. Artemisia held fast to the truth, insisting even as Tassi glared at her and the flesh on her knuckles bulged, "It is true, it is true, it is true!"

Artist's rendering of the *sibille,* a form of torture Artemisia endured during the trial of her rapist. From Gina Siciliano, *I Know What I Am: The Life and Times of Artemisia Gentileschi* (2019). Used with permission.

Tassi was found guilty of rape and of corrupting witnesses to testify falsely on his behalf. He served time in jail before the trial and, after his conviction, was sentenced to exile from Rome, but he never left, because he was a favored painter for the pope.

After the trial, Orazio arranged for Artemisia to marry a Florentine artist named Pierantonio di Vincenzo Stiattesi. The couple moved to Florence, where Artemisia became a popular and successful painter. Her work was supported by the house of Medici, a political dynasty in Italy, and she was held in high esteem.

In 1615 Michaelangelo's nephew Michaelangelo Buonarotti the Younger asked Artemisia to contribute a painting for the ceiling of Casa Buonarotti, a building that was being constructed to honor his famous uncle. Artemisia was quite pregnant when she began her piece and was paid three times more than some of the male artists who were asked to contribute.

Artemisia Gentileschi, *Self-Portrait as the Allegory of Painting (La Pittura),* 1638–39. Oil on canvas, 38 4/5 × 29 3/5 in. Royal Collection.

In 1616 Artemisia was the first woman accepted into the prestigious Accademia delle Arti del Disegno (Academy of the Arts of Drawing). She earned the favor of influential people, including the Grand Duke of Tuscany, the Grand Duchess Christina of Lorraine, and famed astronomer Galileo Galilei.

Artemisia and Stiattesi had five children, but only one, a daughter named Prudenzia (b. 1617), survived to adulthood. During her marriage, Artemisia had an affair with a wealthy man named Francesco Maringhi, which her husband tolerated, presumably because Maringhi financially supported the family. In 1620 Artemisia returned to Rome, where she lived an upper-class lifestyle with her husband, her daughter, and several servants. She then separated from Stiattesi but stayed in Rome until she moved to Venice in 1626. In 1630 she left Venice for Naples, where she lived for the rest of her life, except for an extended trip to London in 1638, when King Charles I invited her to contribute to a fresco at the Queen's House in Greenwich. While there, Artemisia painted her well-known piece *Self-Portrait as the Allegory of Painting* (1638–39). King Charles I was a big fan and added several of Artemisia's pieces to his collection.

Nothing is known about Artemisia's death, though many believe she died in a plague that swept through Naples in 1656. Prudenzia married in 1638 and became an artist like her mother, but there are no known heirs.

After her death, Artemisia's reputation faded. In fact, she was completely ignored by art historians until the early 1900s, when Caravaggio scholar Roberto Longhi discovered her work and learned that many of her pieces had wrongly been attributed to men. Artemisia's 1612 painting *Danae,* for example, had been attributed to Orazio, even though it did not resemble his work and was clearly consistent with Artemisia's style. Artemisia was not credited with the painting until the late 1990s. Another of Artemisia's pieces, *David and Goliath* (1630s), was attributed to a male painter named Giovanni Francesco Guerrieri when it came up for auction in London in 1975, but in 2018, when the piece again became available for sale, this time in Germany, the buyer hired an expert to clean it and discovered Artemisia's signature on David's sword.

Many scholars have written about Artemisia, but not enough has been said about why she was erased from art history. Was she punished for accusing a powerful man of rape? Were her depictions of women as heroic, rebellious, and capable of beheading men with cool indifference too much for the men who controlled the content of art history books? According to Longhi, "there are about fifty-seven [known] works by Artemisia Gentileschi and 94% (forty-nine) feature women as protagonists or equals to men." Maybe men were afraid that Artemisia would influence women to see themselves as strong and independent. No doubt they were also concerned that Artemisia was inspiring other women artists. In 1659 well-known artist Elisabetta Sirani painted *Timocleia of Thebes,* depicting a woman who had just been raped pushing her attacker headfirst into a well. The man's face is filled with terror as he falls helplessly to his fate, legs spread apart, perhaps mimicking the forced position of his victim's legs during the rape.

So where are all the great women artists? Many are still out there, and they deserve to be found and celebrated, especially artists like Artemisia Gentileschi, who dared to see and portray women as men's equals.

Learn More

Dante Alighieri Society Sydney. *The Incredible Life of Artemisia Gentileschi.* YouTube video, 1:18:51, April 11, 2021. https://www.youtube.com/watch?v=r0mYE5DKog4.

Garrard, Mary D. *Artemisia Gentileschi and Feminism in Early Modern Europe.* Renaissance Lives. New York: Reaktion Books, 2020.

Nochlin, Linda. "Why Have There Been No Great Women Artists?" In *Women, Art, and Power and Other Essays,* 145–78. New York: Harper and Row, 1988.

7

HE SAID THAT A WOMAN WAS NOT CAPABLE OF DESIGNING A MACHINE

If you're a woman, you've been underestimated. Whether you fixed a leaky pipe or moved a heavy bureau, someone probably commented about how you couldn't possibly have done it yourself. Stereotypes about women's abilities make it easier for men to take credit for women's work because women are less likely to be believed when they say they did something "manly." Margaret Eloise Knight suffered exactly this type of insult when she designed a machine to manufacture paper bags and the man who stole her invention defended himself by declaring that a woman did not have the capacity to design such a complex machine.

Margaret Knight was born in York, Maine, on February 14, 1838, and raised in nearby New Hampshire. From a young age, Margaret loved using tools and learning how things worked. She was well known among her friends as a talented builder of kites and sleds. She was also a very good student, but her father died when she was a toddler, so she left school at age twelve and worked in a cotton mill to help her mother pay the bills.

The Industrial Revolution was in full swing, so there were plenty of factory jobs around, but conditions were terrible.

Despite her young age, Margaret worked from dawn to dusk at a textile factory for low wages. At work one day, Margaret saw a metal piece break free from a weaving loom and fly like a projectile across the room, hitting a worker. She quickly designed a restraint system to stop the pieces from shooting off and showed it to her boss. He shared it with others, and Margaret's invention was soon adopted by the entire industry. At twelve years old, Margaret was too young to get a patent, so she didn't benefit financially, but the experience taught her the money-making potential of her inventive mind.

Margaret worked at several other factories and taught herself about machines. When the Civil War ended in 1865, she went to work at the Columbia Paper Bag Company in Springfield, Massachusetts, which made paper bags from large sheets of paper. Margaret thought the bags were not well designed because they were flat and couldn't hold much. They also had to be hand-folded, which was inefficient. Margaret was certain she could design a machine that could make and fold bags with flat bottoms.

She started working on drawings and eventually built a wooden prototype of a machine that could cut, fold, and glue flat-bottomed paper bags. She brought it to the factory and showed her boss. He was so impressed that he urged Margaret to bring it to a machinist in Boston so it could be built from sturdy metal rather than wood.

The machinist at the Lincoln and Graham Machine Shop thought Margaret's invention was brilliant. Customers looked on in amazement as she demonstrated how it worked. One man in particular asked Margaret to explain the different parts in detail.

The shop owner told Margaret her machine would be ready in a few weeks. When she returned to pick it up, the same customer who had asked to see the details was there again. Margaret was suspicious and made a mental note of his name when she heard someone call him "Charles."

Margaret knew it was important to get a patent, so she spent months perfecting her drawings before sending in her application and the thirty-five-dollar fee. Weeks later, she received a letter in the mail stating that her application

Sheet 1

Margaret E. Knight

PATENTED JUL 11 1871

116842

Bag Machine

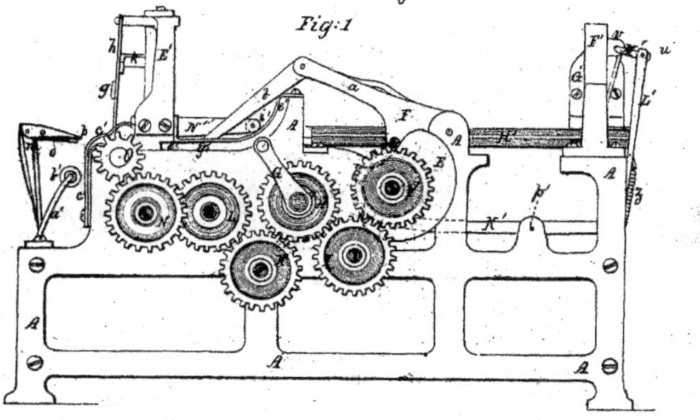

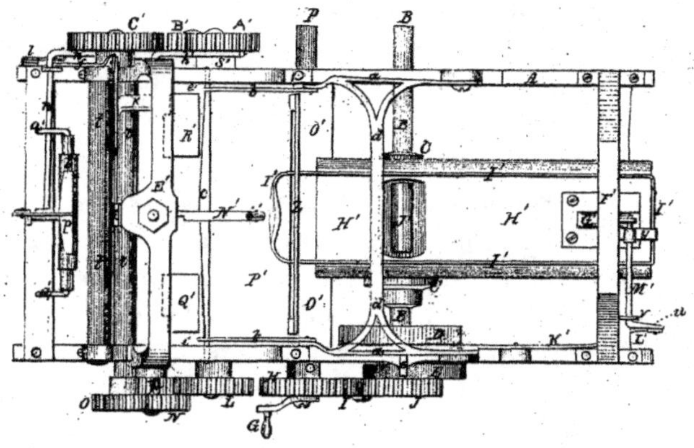

Witnesses

A. C. Bradley

Geo. C. Lambright

Inventor

Margaret E. Knight

By her Attorney

Chas. F. Stansbury

Margaret Knight's patent drawing for her "bag machine." Patent 116842, July 1871. Courtesy US Patent Office.

First Woman Granted an American Patent Is Still at Work on Ingenious Inventions

Margaret in the *Boston Sunday Post Sunday Magazine,* 1912.

had been denied because a man named Charles Annan had already obtained a patent for the same machine. Margaret was furious. She recalled the man named Charles who had spoken to her at the machine shop and decided to fight back.

The letter from the Patent Office said she could appeal the decision by traveling to Washington, DC, and presenting her case to the commissioner of patents. She hired a lawyer and filed an appeal.

The hearing before the commissioner took place in summer 1871. Annan defended himself by testifying that no woman was capable of designing such a complex machine. Margaret responded by producing a large stack of detailed drawings showing the progression of her invention from idea to production. She also had witnesses on her side—her boss at the factory and the machinist who built the metal prototype both testified that Margaret was the true inventor.

The case dragged on for more than two weeks before the commissioner ruled in Margaret's favor. She was the first woman to win a patent infringement case since the Patent Office was established in 1836.

Emboldened by her landmark victory, Margaret started her own business in Hartford, Connecticut, and named it the Eastern Paper Bag Company. She enjoyed a successful career as a business owner and invented nearly a hundred products related to things like automobile engines, shoes, dresses, and window frames. She was granted more than twenty patents during her lifetime.

Margaret died in 1914 at age seventy-six. She was inducted into the National Inventors Hall of Fame in 2006. Her original paper bag machine is still on display at the Smithsonian in Washington, DC.

Margaret's legacy as the first woman to win a case before the commissioner of patents is an important part of her story. In the 1800s, even single women often applied for patents using their husbands' or fathers' names because they had only limited rights. Patent thieves knew this and would steal

Margaret's original machine, on display at the Smithsonian Institution, Washington, DC. Courtesy the Smithsonian Institution.

patents that were filed under a woman's name. Margaret might have filed hers under a man's name, but she had neither a husband nor a father.

When Margaret won her case in 1871, fewer than 2 percent of patents had been granted to women. Today that figure has climbed to only 19 percent, though it's hard to know for sure because the Patent Office doesn't keep statistics on how many women apply for or receive patents. The data that do exist are from studies conducted by private researchers, who guess whether an applicant is female based on the applicant's first name. This isn't good enough. The Patent Office itself should keep track of how many women apply for patents compared to men and how many are granted or denied. So long as women remain unequal under the law, government officials should be measuring the injustices women endure.

Charles Annan knew that Margaret had only limited rights as a woman. Too bad for him that even second-class citizens win sometimes.

Learn More

Petroski, Henry. "The Evolution of the Grocery Bag." *American Scholar* 72, no. 4 (2003): 99–113. https://www.jstor.org/stable/41221195.

Smith, Ryan P. "Meet the Female Inventor behind Mass-Market Paper Bags." *Smithsonian,* March 15, 2018, updated March 28, 2019. https://www.smithsonianmag.com/smithsonian-institution/meet-female-inventor-behind-mass-market-paper-bags-180968469/.

8

THE INVISIBLE WOMAN BEHIND DR. MARTIN LUTHER KING JR.

Have you ever worked really hard on something, only to have nobody notice? It's not unusual in political campaigns for volunteers to work hard while only the politician gets attention. For the most part, volunteers accept invisibility as part of the job, but what if *some* people get recognition, while others don't? And what if the only one who doesn't get recognized is a woman? Such is the story of Anna Arnold Hedgeman, a social justice activist whose work was critical to the success of the March on Washington in 1963, where Dr. Martin Luther King Jr. made his famous "I Have a Dream" speech.

Anna Hedgeman was born in Marshalltown, Iowa, on July 5, 1899, to William James and Marie Ellen Arnold. When they moved to Minnesota a few years later, they were the only Black family in town, but they felt welcome, and Anna's family was actively involved in the community.

After Anna graduated from high school in 1918, she entered Hamline University, a Methodist college in St. Paul, Minnesota. She was the school's first Black student and its first Black graduate when she earned her bachelor's degree in English in 1922. During her time at Hamline, Anna attended a talk by civil rights leader W. E. B. Du Bois, who had helped found the NAACP in 1909. Du Bois inspired Anna to become a teacher and a civil rights activist.

Anna's first job after college was as a teacher of English and history at Rust College, the oldest historically Black college in Mississippi. It was there that she experienced racial segregation for the first time. Anna quit teaching to focus on civil rights.

From 1924 to 1938 she worked as executive director of several segregated branches of the YWCA in New Jersey, Ohio, Pennsylvania, and New York. Anna also worked as a consultant for the Emergency Relief Bureau (later the Department of Welfare) in New York City during the Great Depression, investigating racial issues and underground slavery in the Bronx slave markets. She developed excellent advocacy skills.

As Anna experienced more and more racism and saw the growing discontent among Black people, she became more political, and more militant. This led to her forced resignation as executive director of the Black branch of the Brooklyn YWCA, but it also made Anna even more committed to the cause.

In 1936 Anna married Merritt Hedgeman. The couple moved to Washington, DC, where Anna was appointed executive secretary of the National Council for a Permanent Fair Employment Practices Commission. She stayed for two years before becoming assistant dean of women at Howard University. Anna also served as a consultant to Harry Truman's 1948 presidential campaign and was later hired to work in his administration's Health, Education, and Welfare Department.

In 1954 New York City mayor Robert F. Wagner announced with great fanfare that he was appointing Anna to a cabinet-level position in his administration, but he gave her no such job. Anna mobilized her allies in the Black community and notified the news media. The mayor was shamed into giving Anna a cabinet-level position, though he put her in the basement of City Hall. She served as intermediary between Harlem and City Hall, and attended events for the mayor if he was unavailable. A few years later, Anna took a position in the public relations department of Fuller Products Company,

Anna Arnold Hedgeman at a hospital in Harlem, New York City, 1958, with Governor W. Averill Harriman (*far right*), where Dr. Martin Luther King Jr. was recovering after being stabbed while autographing copies of his new book.

and in 1959 she became associate editor and columnist for the influential Black newspaper the *New York Age*.

After decades of hard work as a social justice activist, Anna was invited to serve on the central organizing committee for the March on Washington, where Dr. King delivered his famous speech. She was the only woman on the committee. Promoted as the March on Washington for Jobs and Freedom, the event was scheduled to take place in front of the Lincoln Memorial on August 28, 1963.

It was a critical time in the civil rights movement, and organizers needed a strong showing. Anna's wealth of experience as an activist made her perfect for the job. She used her connections with the many organizations she had worked with over the years to communicate the importance of high attendance. She brilliantly inspired massive enthusiasm and personally delivered tens of thousands of Black people to the March, making sure they had free transportation and were given food and water upon their arrival. She also persuaded white people to attend by using her position at the National Council of Churches to speak to white Christians about why

Marchers from the National Council of Churches, with which Anna was influential, at the March on Washington, 1963. Photograph by Marion S. Trikosko.

racism was contrary to their religious beliefs. Forty thousand of them showed up.

More than two hundred thousand people attended the March; many were women. In an interview a week before the event, Anna emphasized that the March was about women's suffering too. "Women are the most discriminated against of all the minorities," she told the reporter, but "some of them just don't recognize" that they "suffer from the same prejudice."

Anna had worked especially hard persuading Black women leaders to support the March and assumed they would have a turn at the microphone, but only men were on the list of speakers. Anna was furious. A. Phillip Randolph, who headed the organizing committee, wanted women to stand behind him while he spoke and to bow when he was done. Anna would have none of it. She wrote a note to the committee, saying, "In light of the role of Negro women in the struggle for freedom, it is incredible that no woman should appear as a speaker at the historic March on Washington meeting

Portrait of Anna, by Betsy Graves Reyneau. Reproduced with permission of Peter Fayard. Copyright National Portrait Gallery, Smithsonian Institution.

at the Lincoln Memorial. I would like to make the following suggestion: That a Negro woman makes a brief statement and presents the other heroines. I hope that my memorandum will receive careful consideration."

Anna gave the committee the names of two women she thought would be good speakers. In the end, Daisy Bates was allowed to say a few words, but she was not permitted to make a speech. During Daisy's brief moment onstage, Anna and her female colleagues looked at each other with knowing smiles. As Anna would later write in her autobiography, "we recognized anew that Negro women are second-class citizens in the same way that white women are in our culture."[1]

Anna's vital role as a member of the committee that organized the March on Washington has not been included in the written history; only the men who worked with Anna are credited, including Congressman John Lewis and Dr. King. They are known today as the Big Six, while Anna, the seventh member, is barely known at all.

Anna's experience with the March on Washington shifted her focus to women's rights, and in 1966 she became one of the founders of the National Organization for Women (NOW). Frustrated by the lack of female leadership in the antiracism movement, Anna thought she might find more meaningful opportunities with a women's rights group, but that did not happen. At its first national meeting, NOW's president, Betty Friedan, announced that NOW would not be supporting the Equal Rights Amendment (ERA). Women across the country were furious. How could a women's organization emerge at such a critical time and be *opposed* to women's equality? NOW eventually supported the ERA, but its commitment was lukewarm, until it was too late.

Anna's influence faded after she joined NOW. She died at a Harlem hospital in 1990, at age ninety.

---

1. Paula Giddings, *When and Where I Enter: The Impact of Black Women on Sex and Race in America* (New York: William Morrow, 1984), 316.

Learn More

Hedgeman, Anna. *The Trumpet Sounds: A Memoir of Negro Leadership*. New York: Holt, Rinehart, and Winston, 1964.

Lott, Martha. "The Relationship between the 'Invisibility' of African American Women in the American Civil Rights Movement of the 1950s and 1960s and Their Portrayal in Modern Film." *Journal of Black Studies* 48, no. 4 (2017): 331–54. https://doi.org/10.1177/0021934717696758.

Scanlon, J. *Until There Is Justice: The Life of Anna Arnold Hedgeman*. Oxford: Oxford University Press, 2016.

9

THE PROFESSOR WHO GOT CREDIT FOR HIS STUDENT'S DISCOVERY

If you've ever heard the term *cell receptor* and had no idea what it meant, you're in good company. It refers to the part of a cell's exterior membrane that attaches to molecules, which are the smallest parts of a substance. If a molecule attaches to a cell receptor, the receptor becomes activated and begins communicating with other cells. If it doesn't attach, the receptor does not become activated. For example, if you take vitamin D, it will attach to a vitamin D receptor, which will then signal other cells to increase the absorption of calcium. The fact that cells function this way was not well understood until fairly recently, but as soon as it was, scientists began devoting substantial resources to the task of identifying cell receptors so they could develop new medicines that treat illnesses by working on receptors.

It's a big deal when a new receptor is discovered—awards are often given to the scientists who discover them. In most cases, those people have been men, but a woman discovered the cell receptor for opiates—though only her male boss got the credit, because she was a PhD student at the time. Candace Pert spent the rest of her life making sure people knew that she was the one who had made the discovery.

Candace Pert. Photograph courtesy Michael Ruff. Used with permission.

Candace Pert was born in Manhattan, New York City, on June 26, 1946. She graduated with honors from Bryn Mawr College in 1970 with a degree in biology and entered a PhD program in pharmacology at the Johns Hopkins University, where she worked in a lab under the direction of Solomon Snyder, MD. Candace was eager to work with Snyder because he was doing research to identify cell receptors in the brain, and she was interested in the relationship between mind and body.

Candace was frustrated by the technique Snyder was using to look for brain receptors because she thought it was ineffective and time-consuming. She developed a better technique, known as a receptor-binding assay, which enabled her to examine the selectivity and affinity of a test agent more effectively—meaning she could more quickly identify a new receptor.

Using her new technique, Candace discovered the opiate receptor. It was a very important discovery because it marked the first time a scientist had identified a cell receptor in the brain. In 1973 Snyder published a paper on Candace's discovery in the journal *Science* with Candace listed as second author. Candace received her PhD a year later.

The discovery of the opiate receptor earned the coveted Lasker Award in 1978. Formally known as the Albert Lasker Basic Medical Research Award, the award is given annually to people who make major contributions to medical science. The prize is so prestigious that it is often referred to as the American Nobel Prize, and many recipients go on to win Nobel Prizes.

Though it was Candace who made the discovery, she did not win the Lasker Award; it went to Snyder instead. Candace

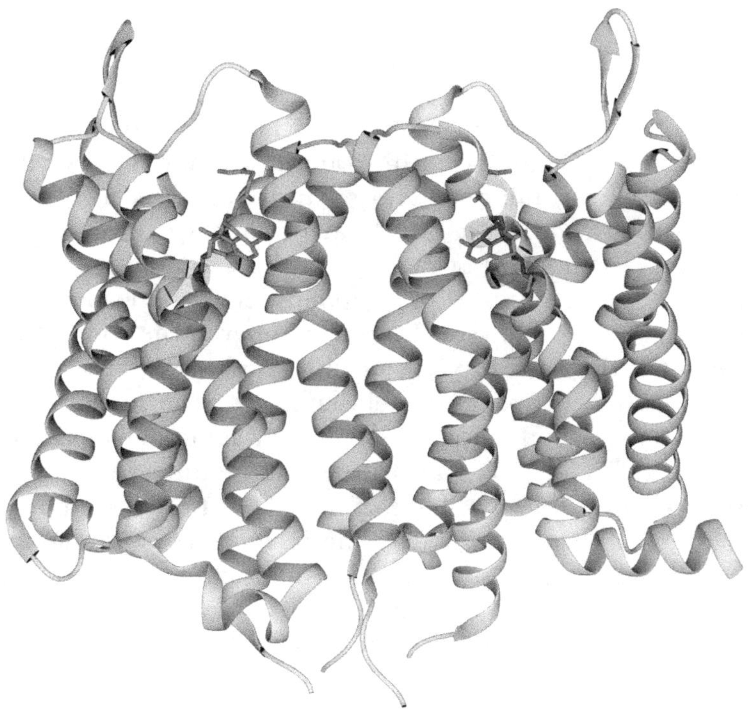

Artist's rendition of an opioid receptor membrane protein. Courtesy Molecular Science/Adobe Stock.

understood that PhD students generally do not win awards for the work they do in someone else's lab, but her situation was unique: she had not simply followed her lab director's instructions—she had invented a better research tool and used it to make the discovery.

Snyder invited Candace to attend the Lasker Award ceremony with him, but she declined. To his credit, Snyder recognized Candace in his acceptance speech, saying, "My own special thanks go to Candace Pert, who, as a graduate student, identified the opiate receptors in my laboratory." Candace was not satisfied. She wrote a letter to Mary Lasker, then head of the Lasker Foundation, explaining how she had developed the receptor-binding assay that enabled her to discover the opiate receptor. Candace's letter was a serious breach of protocol, but she wanted the foundation to know that she was offended. "I played a key role in initiating this research and following it up," she wrote. Her letter accused the foundation of discriminating against her because she was a woman.

Many women scientists came to Candace's defense, though the male-dominated scientific community supported Snyder and said that Candace had no grounds to complain because she was a student. Lasker Award officials responded to Candace's complaint by saying that she did not deserve the award because she was working for Snyder when she made the discovery. But a few years later, a member of the committee that gave the award to Snyder published a letter in *Science* saying, "In retrospect, we feel that it was a significant omission on our part that Dr. Candace Pert was not included. Her graduate student role was the issue at the time; subsequent increased awareness of her major contribution has led us to this revised conclusion. Selecting recipients for prestigious awards is a complex social process in which 'scientific merit,' unfortunately, is often only one of many considerations. Sometimes, serious mistakes are made."[1]

---

1. William Pollin, "Pert and the Lasker Award," letter, *Science,* April 6, 1979, https://www.science.org/doi/10.1126/science.204.4388.8.a.

Candace in her office at the National Institutes of Mental Health. Photograph courtesy Michael Ruff. Used with permission.

Things have not improved much at the Lasker Foundation. A recent study found that between 1946 and 2022, less than 8 percent of Lasker Awards went to women, a percentage that has not changed in more than seventy years. Perhaps the shape of the award needs to change before things get better: at the moment, it's a statue of a mildly clothed (her belly button is visible), headless woman with wings. Maybe more women would win if the statue itself at least conveyed the idea that women *have* brains.[2]

After earning her PhD, Candace moved to the National Institutes of Mental Health (NIMH) Intramural Research Program. She won the coveted Arthur S. Flemming Award for distinguished federal service in the same year that she didn't win the Lasker Award.

In 1983 Candace became the first woman chief of the Section on Brain Biochemistry in the Clinical Neuroscience Branch at the NIMH. She focused her work on neuropeptides (amino acids in the brain that help build proteins) and the immune system and, in 1985, published a well-known paper in the *Journal of Immunology* showing how neuropeptides and their cell receptors represent the "biochemical substrate of emotion." Candace would later explain that this means all cells in the body receive emotional information, making the entire body a kind of "subconscious mind." Her pioneering research on how this works at a molecular level, and how the cellular nature of emotions creates a bridge between mind and body, is widely regarded today as seminal.

Because of her understanding of neuropeptides and cell receptors, Candace studied diseases in terms of how they were affected by these two components. One of the diseases she studied was HIV/AIDS. It was spreading quickly in the 1980s, and Candace wanted to help. In 1986 she discovered a peptide known as peptide T that inhibited the development of AIDS by blocking HIV (the virus that causes AIDS) from attaching to cell receptors. If peptide T could prevent the virus from attaching, she thought, AIDS would never develop as a disease. Her theory proved true to a large extent, and her discovery helped dramatically reduce the amount of virus present in the bodies of HIV patients. Peptide T is still being studied today for its ability to prevent and reverse inflammation and neurodegeneration not only among HIV/AIDS patients but also in patients with stroke

2. For a photo of the headless Lasker Award, see https://laskerfoundation.org/wp-content/uploads/2021/03/top_nominations.jpg.

and brain injury and with dementia, Alzheimer's disease, or Parkinson's disease.

During the course of her career, Candace gained fame as a neuroscientist who uniquely understood the ways that the brain, the glands in the body, and the entire immune system—including all cells—work together in a "bidirectional network of communication" and that the "information 'carriers' are the neuropeptides."[3] Candace's work launched a novel way of thinking about the role of neuropeptides in mind–body medicine. Her work led to a new category of science known as psychoneuroimmunology. Candace's research showed that there is no separation between mind and body, which inspired her to coin the word *bodymind* to emphasize that one's emotions, mind, and consciousness are interconnected with physiology and wellness. This concept is widely accepted today, but it was controversial when Candace first began writing about it in the 1970s.

Candace's work has enhanced our understanding of why practices like meditation, breathing, yoga, and other "alternative" medicine practices are effective at treating emotional and psychological conditions as well as physical and biological diseases. Indeed, the part of the brain that controls breathing contains all the neuropeptides that affect the entire body.

Candace eventually published 252 scientific papers and several books. Brilliant and creative, she continued to focus on peptides and the importance of ensuring that medical professionals and the general public understand the way mind and body work together to restore health and promote wellness. She passed away in 2013, leaving behind a mountain of scholarly work and a well-deserved reputation as a bold, outside-the-box thinker and fearless advocate for women in science and society.

3. http://candacepert.com/articles/the-wisdom-of-the-receptors-neuropeptides-the-emotions-and-the-bodymind/.

Learn More

Candace Pert, http://www.candacepert.com/.

Lasker Foundation, https://laskerfoundation.org/.

Pert, Candace. *Molecules of Emotion: The Science behind Mind–Body Medicine.* New York: Simon and Schuster, 1999.

Pert, Candace B., Michael R. Ruff, Richard J. Weber, and Miles Herkenham. "Neuropeptides and Their Receptors: A Psychosomatic Network." *Journal of Immunology* 135, no. 2 (1985): 820s–26s. https://doi.org/10.4049/jimmunol.135.2.820.

10

ALBERT EINSTEIN'S NOBEL PRIZE BELONGS TO HIS WIFE, TOO

It's one thing to take credit for your wife's work; it's another to suck the life out of her by using her brain to advance your own career and then, once you have all you need, dump her like yesterday's news and marry your cousin. This pretty much sums up what happened to Mileva Marić Einstein, the first wife of renowned theoretical physicist Albert Einstein.

Mileva Marić was born in Austria-Hungary (now Serbia) in 1875 to Marija Ruzić and Miloš Marić. The eldest of three children in a wealthy and respected family, Mileva entered a school for girls in 1886 and learned math from a well-known theoretical physicist, Vladimir Varićak. For high school, Mileva moved to Zurich, Switzerland, but, as a girl, was forbidden to study physics until her father got special permission for her to attend classes with boys. She graduated in 1894, earning the highest possible grades in math and physics. She then entered an all-women university and, after passing her exams, was accepted into medical school at the nearby University of Zurich.

Albert Einstein was born in Germany in March 1879, the eldest of the two children of Hermann and Pauline Einstein. His father founded an electrical manufacturing company; his

Mileva Marić Einstein, 1896.

mother was from a wealthy family. He attended grade school and high school in Germany and excelled at math and physics.

When Albert was fifteen, his father's business failed, and the family moved to Italy, but Albert stayed behind so he could finish high school in Munich. Albert soon quit high school and moved to Switzerland, where, at age sixteen, he took the entrance exam for the prestigious Zurich Polytechnic Institute (ZPI). Although his scores in math and physics were excellent, he failed other subjects and was denied admission. He was advised to attend the Argovian Cantonal School to finish high school before applying again. In 1896, after completing high school at age seventeen with the highest grades in math and physics, Albert was accepted into a four-year program at ZPI that would allow him to become a teacher of math and physics.

That same year, at age twenty, Mileva left medical school. She preferred math and physics and transferred from the

University of Zurich to the same program as Albert at ZPI. Mileva was the lone woman among six students in a program that restricted admissions of women and accepted only the most talented female applicants.

Mileva and Albert quickly became close intellectual friends and, after a while, romantic partners. They studied and worked together constantly. Mileva's friends Helene Kaufler-Savić and Milan Bota spoke of how Albert was always at the pension house for women where Mileva lived while attending ZPI.

Mileva was painfully shy, organized, and methodological, whereas Albert was more outgoing and undisciplined. He attended few classes because he thought the course material was uninteresting or outdated.

In late 1897 Mileva left ZPI to study for a few months at Heidelberg University in Germany under the guidance of Philipp Lenard, who would win the Nobel Prize in Physics in 1905. She excitedly wrote to Albert about Lenard's work, and Albert told Mileva that he was especially interested in learning more about Lenard's research on light and electrons.

Albert often relied on Mileva to help him with his studies and ideas. In a letter dated August 1899, he wrote, "When I read Helmholtz for the first time, it seemed so odd that you were not at my side and today, this is not getting better. I find the work we do together very good, healing and also easier." On October 2, 1899, he wrote, "I miss having you nearby to kindly keep me in check and prevent me from meandering."

At the conclusion of their studies in 1900, Mileva's grade point average was 4.0 out of 5.0; Albert's was 4.9. The other students all received scores above 5.0. Mileva and Albert each received a 10 in experimental physics. In theoretical physics, Albert received a 10, Mileva a 9. Nonetheless, when the students were given their final oral exams by a male instructor in July 1900, all the men passed, while Mileva failed, which meant she would not graduate. Mileva returned to Serbia to study and prepare to retake her oral exam.

Albert graduated but could not find a job. All the other male students got teaching appointments, but Albert did not.

The couple wanted to get married, but Albert refused to marry before he had a respectable job. He was also feeling resistance from his family—his mother thought Mileva was too old (she was less than three years older); she also said that Mileva was not a good fit because she was too intellectual and neither Jewish nor German.

While Mileva studied in Serbia, Albert stayed in Italy with his family. Albert wrote to Mileva often while they were apart. In one letter from September 1900, he said, "I look forward to resume our new common work. You must now continue with your research. How proud I will be to have a doctor for my spouse when I'll only be an ordinary man." In another letter the same year, he told Mileva that she was "a creature who is my equal."

The couple reunited briefly in Zurich in October 1900. Two months later, Albert published his first scientific paper. It was on capillarity, which refers to the rate at which a liquid moves across a surface. The paper was signed only by Albert, though Mileva's role as coauthor was noted in letters Albert wrote to Mileva prior to publication, describing it as "our" paper and saying "we" asked for comments from colleagues.

Before retaking her oral exam, Mileva traveled to Italy to see Albert in April 1901 and became pregnant. She returned to Zurich in July 1901 to retake her exam but, again, failed. She told Albert that she would no longer pursue her degree and went back to Serbia, where she gave birth to a baby girl in January 1902. Little is known about the child, but Mileva did not have the baby with her when she moved to Switzerland with Albert in fall 1902. Many believe the child lived for a while with Mileva's parents, then was given up for adoption. Albert's father meanwhile had given Albert permission to marry Mileva right before he died in 1902. In that same year, Albert's friend's father helped Albert get a job at the Patent Office in Bern, Switzerland. Now employed, Albert married Mileva in January 1903, and the couple settled in a small apartment in Bern.

Albert worked eight hours a day, six days a week as a clerk at the Patent Office and spent evenings working with Mileva on math and physics problems. A physics professor named

Đorđe Krstić, who spent fifty years researching Mileva's life, said that Mileva's brother Miloš visited the couple often and talked about seeing them sitting together at night, calculating, reading, debating, and working on physics problems. Other people who knew the couple said the same thing.

The couple's first son, Hans-Albert, was born in May 1904. Albert received his PhD from the University of Zurich the following year. His dissertation was published in 1905 in the prestigious journal *Annals of Physics* and was titled "A New Determination of Molecular Dimensions," a topic that Mileva had also studied and had discussed with Albert in written correspondence. Albert published four additional academic papers in 1905 in the same journal. Popularly known as comprising Albert's *annus mirabilis* (miracle year), his 1905 papers are all significant to our understanding of modern physics.

The first "miracle year" paper was about light and the photoelectric effect. At the time, scientists believed that light was made up of waves, but Albert showed that light was made up of particles called photons and that photons could knock an electron off an atom to create an electric current. This was the same topic Mileva had studied under the direction of Lenard when she was at Heidelberg University. Albert had told Mileva how interested he was in Lenard's work and later told his biographer that his paper on the photoelectric effect had taken five years to complete, which means that he developed it between 1900 and 1905, years during which he was working and studying with Mileva.

Albert's second paper was about the existence of atoms and molecules. He theorized that particles did not move randomly in water and that their movement was predictable because water is made up of atoms that cause particles to jiggle. Again, this was a topic Albert discussed and debated with Mileva.

His third paper was on electrodynamics and the theory of special relativity, which essentially means that observations about things that happen in the world are affected by where they occur and the location and movement of the observer and the observed; in other words, everything is relative. For example, if two conductors on two different trains in two different countries are asked to start moving at the same time, they will actually start moving at different times based on where they are located, where we are located, and whether we are moving when the trains start moving. This theory was the basis for Albert's fourth paper, which produced the famous equation $E = mc^2$, or energy equals mass times the speed of light squared. Simply put, it means that all mass is energy and all energy is mass. In Albert's letters to Mileva, he described special relativity as "our" work, and he told many people that his papers on special relativity and $E = mc^2$ were the culmination of seven years' work, which means they were developed between 1898 and 1905, a period of time when he was working and studying with Mileva.

After Albert's 1905 papers were published, the couple took a vacation to visit Mileva's family and friends in Serbia. They visited Serbia many times over the next several years, and the people they visited later reported that the couple often spoke about Albert's 1905 papers as a joint collaboration with Mileva.

The 1905 papers were so groundbreaking that the scientific community did not immediately appreciate their significance, so Albert and Mileva continued with their lives. Mileva also worked with others while Albert stayed at his job at the Patent Office. In 1908 Mileva coinvented a highly sensitive voltmeter with a scientist named Conrad Habicht, but she declined to put her name on the patent. Instead, it was registered under Conrad's and Albert's names. Albert had nothing to do with the invention, but his name was added because he was familiar with the patent process and agreed to take responsibility for describing the device accurately in the application. When Habicht asked Mileva why she refused to put her name on the patent, she replied that it was not necessary because she and Albert were "one stone," meaning the work of one was the work of the other.

Albert was finally offered a teaching position in 1908 at Bern University, though it was unpaid. By the end of 1908, Albert was becoming famous for his 1905 papers, and the University of Zurich hired him as a paid teacher in 1909.

Mileva was proud of Albert's growing success and even wrote some of his lecture notes for him, though she told a friend that she was worried his fame was affecting his humanity, adding, "With all this fame, he has little time for his wife. . . . What is there to say, with notoriety, one gets the pearl, the other the shell."

The couple's second son, Eduard, was born in 1910. Later that same year, the family moved to Prague after Albert was offered a full professorship at the University of Prague. Mileva was still involved in Albert's work, and in 1910 she even responded in writing to a question renowned physicist Max Planck had posed to Albert, though she signed Albert's name.

Albert and Mileva were still working together in 1912, but things fell apart when Albert visited his family in Berlin and began a sexual relationship with his cousin Elsa Löwenthal. Albert and Mileva separated in 1914, and Albert moved to Berlin, where he began teaching at the University of Berlin. Mileva stayed with the children and barely communicated with Albert, except about family matters. Albert asked Mileva for a divorce in 1916 so he could marry Elsa, but Mileva refused. Albert agreed to stay married to Mileva, but only if she complied with certain conditions: he would show her no affection, and she would show none to him; Mileva would cook and clean for Albert but not sit with him at dinner or talk to him about his work; Mileva would leave the room at his request and not disparage him in front of the children. Mileva agreed to the conditions, but the marriage did not last, and Albert eventually demanded a divorce.

In his 1918 divorce proposal, Albert promised Mileva his Nobel Prize money if he were to win any in the future. That he specifically offered her his Nobel Prize money is interesting because if it were just an issue of sharing his future wealth with Mileva and the children, he simply could have promised to give her more money if his income increased. One explanation for why Albert promised Mileva his Nobel Prize money in particular is because it was in exchange for Mileva staying quiet about her involvement in his work.

The divorce became final in 1919, and in 1921 Albert won the Nobel Prize for his 1905 paper on the photoelectric effect. As promised, he did give the prize money to Mileva, but when he later wrote his will, he said his sons should get the money. Mileva reminded him that he had already given the money to her, and she apparently threatened to speak publicly about her role in Albert's work, because he responded, "You made me laugh when you started threatening me with your recollections."[1] He said that nobody would believe her because she was an insignificant person and that she should just remain humble and silent. Mileva did remain silent, though she would later tell people that Albert ruined her life.

Albert never published anything as monumental as his 1905 papers. In fact, after he divorced Mileva, he often asked for help from others to solve math problems and sometimes seemed not to fully understand the significance of his own work. For example, he said in 1934 that atomic energy was impossible, even though $E = mc^2$ is the foundation for scientists' understanding of how atomic energy works. Albert also notoriously resisted the idea of quantum mechanics, which is widely accepted today as a fundamental theory of nature, and it was his paper on the photoelectric effect, for which he won the Nobel Prize, that provided the foundation for quantum mechanics.

Albert made serious mistakes in his work after he left Mileva. He published a paper in 1917, changing the equation for general relativity in a way that appeared to show that the universe was static rather than expanding. When Belgian physicist Georges Lemaître developed a model proving that the universe is expanding, Albert admonished him publicly, saying that his calculations were correct, but his physics was "abominable." Albert was quickly proved wrong.

As late as 1936, Albert was making statements and producing work that other scientists found lacking. He rejected the idea of black holes, a theory widely accepted today, and in a paper on gravitational lensing, which is a way of measuring

---

1. Pauline Gagnon, "The Forgotten Life of Einstein's First Wife," *Scientific American Guest Blog*, December 19, 2016, https://blogs.scientificamerican.com/guest-blog/the-forgotten-life-of-einsteins-first-wife/.

Serbian postage stamp issued in Mileva's honor, 2014.

the distribution of mass in the universe, he claimed that only stars can bend light in a manner that makes matter measurable. His mathematical work on the topic was described as "near disastrous."

Despite his many failings, Albert's career and reputation grew, while Mileva lived in obscurity and poverty. She stayed in Zurich and dedicated her life to caring for her son Eduard, who developed schizophrenia in 1930, at age twenty, and eventually became institutionalized. Albert, meanwhile, became a philanderer who openly dated many other women during his marriage to Elsa. He moved to the United States in 1932 and took a position at Princeton University. Aside from a brief return to Belgium, he lived in New Jersey for the rest of his life.

Mileva died in 1948 at age seventy-two. Albert died in 1955 at age seventy-six.

After Albert died, Frieda, the first wife of Albert and Mileva's son Hans-Albert, attempted to publish a collection of letters she discovered in Mileva's Zurich apartment. The letters were from Albert to Mileva and contained numerous references to Mileva as a contributor to Albert's work. When lawyers for Albert's estate, Helen Dukas and Otto Nathan, learned that Frieda was trying to publish the letters, they went to court to keep them secret. They prevailed at the time, but many of the letters were made public in 1986.

In one letter, dated March 27, 1901, Albert writes to Mileva about their work on relative motion: "How happy I will be when the two of us together will have brought our work on relative motion to a victorious conclusion." This was written at a time when Albert knew Mileva had just given birth to their illegitimate daughter. Perhaps he was wooing Mileva with a promise of fame and glory for both of them, in the hope he could persuade her to give up their child for adoption, as it was scandalous at the time to have an illegitimate child. Maybe Albert was worried he would not be considered morally worthy of the Nobel Prize unless the child disappeared. Regardless, he was explicit that it was *their* work on relative motion that would soon come to a "victorious conclusion," and the letter was written after Albert spent years working with Mileva on math and physics problems. What was Mileva doing while they were working together if not contributing to Albert's work?

Mileva herself never publicly claimed credit for Albert's work, but she did talk about the issue privately. Her friend Milana Bota told a reporter in 1929 to talk to Mileva about special relativity because Mileva was involved in the discovery. Mileva later wrote to another friend, Helene Savic, "Publications do not suit my nature at all, but I believe that all that was for Milana's joy, and that she probably thought that this would also be a joy for me, as I can only suppose that she wanted to help me receive some public rights with regard to Einstein."

Other evidence similarly shows Mileva's involvement in Albert's work:

- During a meeting with fellow intellectuals, Albert said, "I need my wife. She solves for me all my mathematical problems."[2]
- Albert's friends reported that he said to them about Mileva, "She is my genius inspirer, my protector; without her my work would never have been started or finished."[3]
- Mileva's father told several people that Mileva said to him in 1905 about work she was doing with Albert, "Before our departure [for Serbia] we finished important scientific work which will make my husband known around the world."[4]
- The Einsteins' eldest son, Hans, often talked about seeing his parents working together at night at the same table.
- The original manuscript for Albert's theory of special relativity was signed by him and Mileva, but when it was submitted for publication, Mileva's name was removed, even though historians agree that Mileva worked late into the night for many days to check calculations and review the article for errors before it was submitted.
- Albert asked Mileva to research and advise him on scientific topics. For example, in a letter dated March 27, 1901, Albert wrote to Mileva about the theory of relativity and included complex mathematical equations along with a long narrative about a question he hoped to solve with Mileva's help. He said, "I burn with desire to make a gigantic step in the exploration of the nature of latent heat. Don't forget to look up to what extent glass obeys the law of Dulong and Petit."

2. Gagnon, "Forgotten Life of Einstein's First Wife."
3. "Mileva Maric-Einstein," History of Scientific Women, https://scientificwomen.net/women/maric-einstein-mileva-62.
4. Gagnon, "Forgotten Life of Einstein's First Wife."

- In a letter dated April 15, 1901, Albert wrote to Mileva about a new idea he had pertaining to "our theory of molecular forces" and how it might apply to gases. He explained his idea in scientific detail and included complex mathematical formulas. He then asked Mileva to send him one of her books on the topic.
- In a letter dated April 30, 1901, Albert wrote to Mileva that he was thinking about "our investigation" and was wondering whether "our conservative molecular forces [theory] will hold good for gases as well."

It seems obvious that Albert's use of the word "our" when writing to Mileva about his papers on capillarity, special relativity, and molecular forces was an expression of scientific collaboration. Though some have argued that he was merely being solicitous or romantic, he used "I" and "me" when writing to Mileva about another paper he was working on during the same time period, involving thermodynamics.

It's impossible to know how much of Mileva's work contributed to Albert's, but she was indisputably an important part of his success. Yet Albert downplayed and belittled Mileva's involvement after he published his 1905 papers. That he may have intentionally tried to hide Mileva's role in his work is consistent with his reputation for unapologetically failing to credit other scientists and making his work seem more original than it really was.

For example, in his 1905 Nobel Prize–winning paper on the photoelectric effect, Albert describes how when light interacts with metal, it releases photons, and when an atom in metal absorbs a photon, it emits an electron with a measurable amount of energy. This discovery paved the way for the invention of electronic devices and other technologies that require the timed emission of electrons, but it was not Albert who discovered it. Lenard discovered the same thing much earlier, and Mileva had studied under Lenard at Heidelberg University and communicated in writing with Albert about Lenard's work. Albert even wrote to Mileva about his excitement after reading Lenard's work in May 1901, saying, "I have just read a marvelous paper by Lenard on the production of cathode rays by ultraviolet light. Under the influence of this beautiful piece of work, I am filled with such happiness." Yet Albert did not mention Lenard or his work in his Nobel Prize–winning paper. The photoelectric effect had also been described previously by well-known physicist Max Planck, but again, Albert didn't cite him.

Albert's paper on special relativity was also not entirely his idea. Special relativity, sometimes known as spacetime, explains how time and space are related and how the speed of an object in motion affects its mass as well as how it is experienced by observers. Albert claimed publicly that he conceived the idea for special relativity when it came rushing into his mind one day, but in fact, it had been described by many scientists before him, including Olinto De Pretto and Michele Besso. Albert cited Besso in his paper, but not De Pretto, who originated the idea. Hendrik Lorentz and Jules Henri Poincaré had also published papers on the subject, but Albert did not cite them either. When confronted, Albert claimed he knew nothing about Poincaré's work, but Poincaré was a well-known, brilliant mathematician and physicist whose work was widely published between 1889 and 1905.

Albert has also been accused of plagiarizing David Hilbert's work after Hilbert gave a talk on November 20, 1915, in Göttingen, Germany, demonstrating the equation for general relativity. Albert described the exact same equation five days later, but he did not cite Hilbert. He said he discovered the formula on his own, yet Hilbert and Albert had communicated about the issue in the weeks and months before Hilbert's talk. Each man was trying to come up with the correct equation, and they discussed their concerns with each other's ideas when the equations they were sending back and forth seemed inadequate. During his November 20 talk, Hilbert acknowledged Albert and praised his "ingenious methods" for addressing issues in their struggle to solve the equation. Albert, by contrast, did not credit Hilbert when he spoke about the same equation five days later.

Albert even boasted about not giving credit to other scientists, claiming he saw no reason to include a "pedantic review" of prior research on the topics about which he was writing. Highly regarded scientists who have criticized Albert and even called him a plagiarist include Max Born, James MacKaye, G. Burniston Brown, and Charles Nordman.

Albert Einstein was by all accounts a brilliant physicist, but he disrespected some of his fellow male scientists just as he disrespected Mileva. In one letter from 1900, he even referred to Mileva as his "little Negro girl." Unlike the men who openly criticized Albert, Mileva stayed silent. Some say that this is because Albert told Mileva that their work would never be published or win a Nobel Prize if a woman's name was on it and that she agreed to give him sole credit to improve their chances of success. Retired history professor Radmila Milentijević, who published a comprehensive biography of Mileva in 2015, thinks maybe Mileva was being magnanimous simply because she loved Albert. Another possibility is that Albert was a controlling narcissist who manipulated Mileva to a point where she felt weak and unworthy. Regardless, there can be little doubt that Mileva Marić Einstein's story would be a very different one indeed if she had been a man.

Learn More

Asmodelle, Estelle. "The Collaboration of Mileva Maric and Albert Einstein." *Asian Journal of Physics* 24, no. 5 (2015).

Gagnon, Pauline. "The Forgotten Life of Einstein's First Wife." *Scientific American Guest Blog,* December 19, 2016. https://blogs.scientificamerican.com/guest-blog/the-forgotten-life-of-einsteins-first-wife/.

11

A WOMAN, NOT TWO MEN, DISPROVED CONSERVATION OF PARITY

Girls in early twentieth-century China had limited access to education, but one little girl's father wanted to change things, so he built a school for them—and guess what happened? His daughter became a world-renowned physicist whose work won the Nobel Prize. That's the happy part of the story. The unhappy part is that her prize went to two men.

Dubbed the First Lady of Physics, the Chinese Marie Curie, and the Queen of Nuclear Research, Chien-Shiung Wu was born in China on May 31, 1912. Chien-Shiung was the second of three children; her mother was a teacher, her father an engineer who read Chien-Shiung scientific journals rather than children's stories. He founded the Mingde School for girls to ensure that his daughter would get a good education.

At age ten, Chien-Shiung moved away from home to attend a high school where she was able to study math and physics. In 1929 she graduated at the top of her class and enrolled at the National Central University in Nanjing. At first she majored in math, but then switched to physics. After graduation, she became a researcher at the Institute of Physics of

The Mingde Junior High School, founded by Chien-Shiung's father to educate girls; Chien-Shiung attended as a child. Courtesy 白色瑰宝. Reproduced under a Creative Commons Attribution-Share Alike 4.0 International license, https://creativecommons.org/licenses/by-sa/4.0/deed.en.

the Academia Sinica in Taiwan. Her female supervisor had graduated from the University of Michigan with a PhD in physics; she urged Chien-Shiung to study at Michigan too.

Chien-Shiung was accepted into a PhD program at Michigan and left China for the United States in 1936. On her way, she visited the University of California, Berkeley, where she met a physicist named Luke Chia-Liu Yuan, who would become her husband. She was also introduced to physicist Ernest O. Lawrence, who was the director of Berkeley's Radiation Laboratory. Chien-Shiung was interested in Lawrence's work on particle acceleration (for which he would later win a Nobel Prize) and decided to study at Berkeley after learning that women were segregated from men at Michigan and were not allowed to use the school's front entrance. Chien-Shiung was such a highly qualified student that she was offered a place in the PhD program at Berkeley, even though the semester was well under way.

Chien-Shiung focused her studies on beta decay. She worked under the direction of Lawrence and famed Italian physicist Emilio Segrè, who compared Chien-Shiung to Marie Curie. Then known as "Gee," Chien-Shiung completed her PhD in 1940 after presenting her thesis on nuclear fission,

Chien-Shiung at Columbia University, 1963. Courtesy the Smithsonian Institution.

beta decay, and radioactive isotopes. After graduation, she remained at the Radiation Laboratory as a postdoctoral fellow.

In 1942, Chien-Shiung and Yuan got married and moved to the East Coast, where Chien-Shiung was hired as an assistant professor of physics at Smith College in Northampton, Massachusetts. Chien-Shiung liked teaching but was unhappy at Smith because it had no research lab, so she accepted a position at Princeton University in New Jersey, where she served as the first female faculty member in the physics department.

In 1944 Chien-Shiung was invited to work on the Manhattan Project, a classified government program that developed nuclear weapons during World War II. German scientists had already developed nuclear technology, and American government officials, along with leaders of other European nations, were concerned that Hitler was preparing to use it to create nuclear weapons. Chien-Shiung worked on a device that could detect the presence of radiation and helped scientists produce uranium in large quantities. She traveled to New York during the week to work on the Manhattan Project and returned to Princeton on the weekends.

In 1945 Chien-Shiung left Princeton for a professorship at Columbia University and moved to Manhattan, where she gave birth to a son in 1947. In 1952 Chien-Shiung became the first woman at Columbia to be granted tenure as a physics professor.

At Columbia, Chien-Shiung focused on Enrico Fermi's work on beta decay after another physicist raised questions about his results. He was unable to prove that beta decay produced electrons, neutrinos, and positrons, which are the small particles that make up atoms. Chien-Shiung designed studies that proved Fermi was correct.

Chien-Shiung quickly earned a reputation as the world's leading expert on beta decay, which led other scientists to seek her guidance. In the mid-1950s, two physicists named Tsung-Dao Lee and Chen-Ning Yang told Chien-Shiung that they had doubts about the validity of a scientific concept known as conservation of parity. Conservation of parity refers to the way particles interact and holds that overall parity always remains the same, meaning that the total energy of the particles is conserved during their interactions. Lee and

Yang had conducted many theoretical experiments that led them to believe that conservation of parity was not valid for weak interactions, such as when beta decay happens, but they needed an experimental physicist to design a study to prove their theory. They turned to Chien-Shiung for help.

Chien-Shiung knew that she could design an experiment to help the men. It required special equipment, so she traveled to Washington, DC, where there was a lab that had what she needed. By 1957 Chien-Shiung had the results the men were hoping for. Her experiment proved that conservation of parity was invalid when applied to beta decay. Her findings shocked the scientific community because they not only invalidated a foundational theory in physics but also enabled scientists to distinguish between matter and antimatter, which led to the development of what is known today as the standard model. The standard model refers to the way three of the four known fundamental forces in nature—electromagnetics, weak interactions, and strong interactions (but not gravity)—function in the universe.

Chien-Shiung's experiment was so significant that it won a Nobel Prize in 1957, but the prize went to Yang and Lee for their theoretical work, rather than to Chien-Shiung for the brilliant experiment she designed that proved the men's theory. Yang and Lee thanked her in their speeches, but Chien-Shiung was ignored by the Nobel Committee. Nobel laureate Jack Steinberger called the decision not to recognize Chien-Shiung the biggest mistake the Nobel Committee had ever made.

That the committee chose to honor the male theoretical physicists rather than the woman who proved the men's theory stands in stark contrast to the Nobel Committee's decision to do the opposite in Lise Meitner's case (see chapter 2). Lise was the theoretical physicist who conceived the idea of nuclear fission, but the Nobel Prize for that discovery went to a male scientist named Otto Hahn, who had carried out the experiment that proved her theory. It didn't matter to the Nobel Committee that it was Lise who both designed the experiment that Hahn carried out *and* came up with the theoretical explanation for Hahn's results.

President Gerald Ford presenting Chien-Shiung Wu with the National Medal of Science in the East Room, White House, October 18, 1976. From the collections of the Gerald R. Ford Presidential Library and Museum, operated by the National Archives and Records Administration.

Chien-Shiung made many important discoveries after the Nobel Prize debacle and became known as the best experimental physicist in the world. She was awarded the Comstock Prize in Physics in 1964, the National Medal of Science in 1975, and the Wolf Prize in Physics in 1978. Chien-Shiung also became an outspoken advocate for women, famously quipping at a conference at the Massachusetts Institute of Technology in 1964 that "atoms and nuclei and mathematical symbols do not have a preference for masculine rather than feminine treatment." In 1975 Chien-Shiung was named the first female president of the American Physical Society. In 1989, at age seventy-seven, she protested the Tiananmen Square Massacre. The following year, an asteroid was named in her honor.

Chien-Shiung died in 1997 at age eighty-four, after suffering a stroke. Her ashes are buried in the courtyard of the

Mingde School in China—a special place built many years ago by a loving father who just wanted his little girl to learn.

Learn More

Chiang Tsai-Chien. *Madame Wu Chien-Shiung: The First Lady of Physics Research*. Singapore: World Scientific, 2013.

12

AUGUSTE RODIN GASLIT AND COPIED THE ARTWORK OF HIS STUDENT LOVER

It's hardly news that art students often mimic their teachers' styles, but things can get funky when the student starts to outshine the teacher. Such is the tale of a woman named Camille Claudel, whose world-famous artist-teacher Auguste Rodin controlled and manipulated her and shamelessly took credit for her work.

Camille Claudel was born in a small village in northern France on December 8, 1864. The eldest of three children in a middle-class family, her father, Louis Prosper Claudel, was a banker, and her mother, Louise Athanaïse Cécile Cerveaux Claudel, was a homemaker. Camille was formally educated until age twelve, when her family moved to a different part of France, where Camille began making sculptures out of local clay. Though she was young and had no training, she was passionate about art. Her mother disapproved, calling sculpting "unladylike." Camille's father, by contrast, was supportive. He showed her art to a neighbor, well-known sculptor and art teacher Alfred Boucher, and asked him to assess her abilities. Boucher said Camille was talented and recommended that her family support her career as an artist.

Camille Claudel, 1884. Courtesy César.

In 1881 Camille enrolled at the Académie Colarossi in Paris—one of the only art schools open to women that also used male nudes as models. Camille studied there under Boucher's direction.

Though she was still living at home in 1882, Camille and three other women students rented a sculpting studio in Paris. That same year, Boucher told Camille that he was moving to Italy and that his colleague Auguste Rodin would take over instruction of his students.

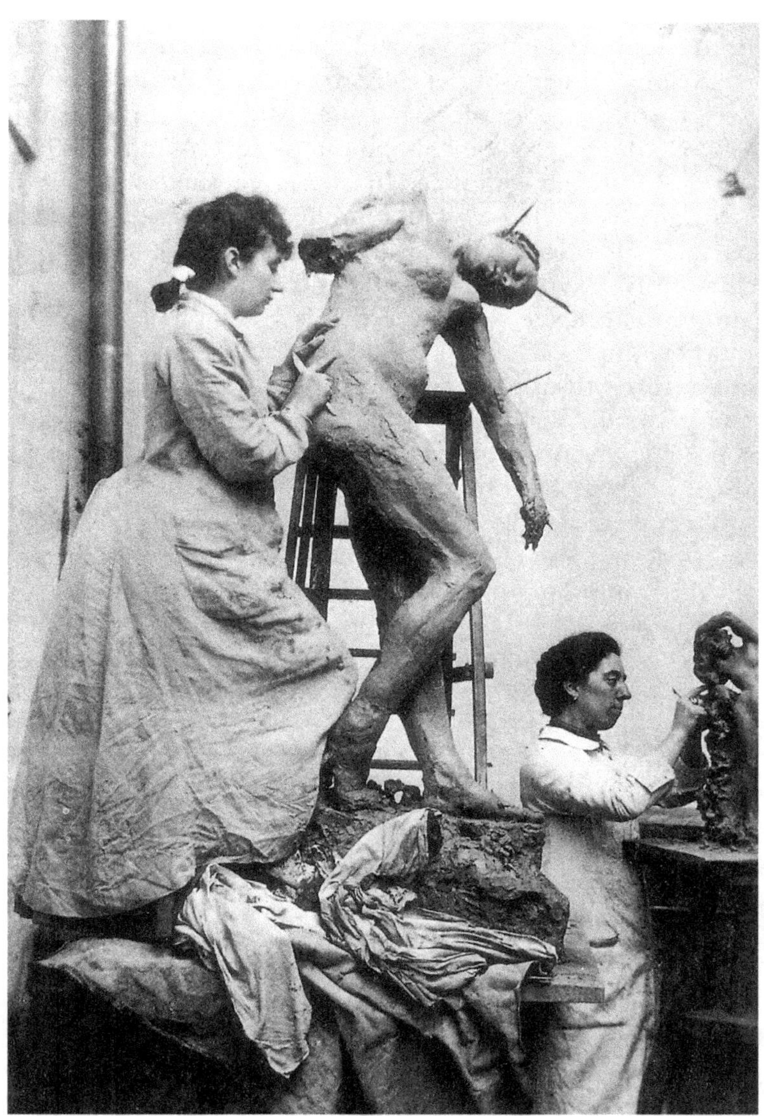

Camille in her Paris studio, mid-1880s, with fellow artist Jessie Lipscomb. Courtesy William Elborne.

Camille became Rodin's student in 1883, when she was nineteen and he was forty-two. Rodin was impressed and invited Camille to work directly with him as his apprentice. Rodin was already famous, as he had been commissioned in 1880 by France's undersecretary of the Ministry of Fine Arts to sculpt a portal for a planned Museum of Decorative Arts. His design included his famous piece *The Thinker* (1904), which Rodin had completed in its original small size in 1881.

Rodin worked closely with Camille, even having her sculpt parts of his most famous works, such as *The Gates of Hell* (1880–1917). Camille was initially Rodin's assistant, model, and muse, but she soon became his lover. When Camille's mother found out about the relationship, she was furious. She already disapproved of Camille working as a sculptor and generally disliked Camille because she had wanted a son. When she heard about Camille's involvement with Rodin, she kicked her out of the house.

Camille remained in a relationship with Rodin for more than a decade and worked primarily on his sculptures, though she did some of her own work, too. Rodin publicly supported Camille when she had exhibitions between 1882 and 1889, but more often than not, he had her work on his pieces, usually sculpting hands and feet. Rodin was highly regarded for the hands and feet of his sculptures, but he did not give credit to Camille.

Over time, Camille fell more deeply in love with Rodin. He financially supported her but lived with another woman. He promised Camille that they would one day be together, even signing a pledge to be faithful to her despite his relationship with a longtime lover. Camille begged him to leave her, but he refused. Camille grew more and more distraught, especially after she became pregnant in 1892 and Rodin insisted that she have an abortion. When Camille became pregnant again, and again he made her terminate the pregnancy, she realized that Rodin would never leave his partner. She told him the relationship was over, though Rodin continued to support her.

Camille was determined to distinguish herself as an artist. She knew her style was often compared to Rodin's, so she

Camille Claudel, *The Mature Age,* 1899. Bronze cast. Musée D'Orsay. Courtesy Thibsweb.

focused on creating pieces that would set her apart. Soon after their breakup, she sculpted some of her most famous pieces, including *The Waltz* (1889–1905) and *The Mature Age* (1899). *The Mature Age* was commissioned by the French state, initially with Rodin's support. It depicts an old man being embraced by an old woman, while a young woman kneels behind the man, reaching for his outstretched hand. When Rodin saw the piece, he was furious. He told Camille it was obviously him and his partner, with Camille the young woman kneeling behind. He told her to destroy it, as it would ruin his reputation, but she refused. Rodin retaliated by cutting off financial and public support. The French government then canceled its funding for *The Mature Age* and never again commissioned Camille's work.

Camille's art became more intense after she left Rodin. Free from his control, she could express herself more vividly, often in ways that were sensual and that challenged society's expectations of women.

Meanwhile, Rodin was taking credit for Camille's work. He even signed his name to some of her pieces and copied her designs. When Camille called him out, he retaliated by further alienating her from the art world. Camille was feeling increasingly isolated as a woman in an artistic community dominated by men, at one point saying that she wanted to change her career because "this unfortunate art is made for long beards and ugly faces rather than for a relatively well-endowed woman."

Camille believed that Rodin was conspiring with others to ruin her reputation. By 1905 she was living alone, financially ruined. She was angry and frustrated that Rodin was still copying her sculptures, so she destroyed many of her pieces to stop him from plagiarizing her work. Camille's father continued to support her financially, but within days of his death in 1913, her brother signed papers admitting her to a psychiatric hospital. At the time, a woman could be institutionalized based solely on a man's claim that she was mentally ill. Camille's brother insisted that she was ill, though the doctors disagreed and repeatedly told Camille's family that she did not need to be in a mental hospital. Some speculate that Rodin paid Camille's brother to put her into an asylum, and Camille herself said that Rodin met with her family in Paris to arrange her psychiatric commitment.

To keep Camille institutionalized, the doctors needed a diagnosis. They chose "persecution delirium mostly based upon false interpretations and imagination." The persecution part was true. Rodin was jealous and angry that Camille had left him, and he was worried that she would publicly reveal that she'd done some of the work on his pieces and that he'd copied her designs. By refusing to financially support Camille and using his influence to institutionalize her, Rodin made sure she would not have enough money to make sculptures, and that if she told people he'd copied her art, nobody would believe her.

Camille's mother never visited her in the asylum. Her brother visited a few times; her sister only once. Friends who visited knew Camille was not mentally ill and did not need to be in a hospital. Camille understood very well what was going on, writing in her diary, "I am scared; I don't know what is going to happen to me. What was the point of working so hard and of being talented, to be rewarded like this? Never a penny, tormented all my life. It is horrible; one cannot imagine it."

Camille died in 1943 after living for thirty years in an asylum. Her family did not claim the body, and she was buried in a communal grave.

Some of Camille's pieces today sell for more than Rodin's, and many art historians believe that Camille was a better sculptor than Rodin because her work is more virile and emotional, whereas Rodin's is delicate and stilted.

Although Rodin succeeded in destroying Camille financially and emotionally, he did not prevent the public from eventually learning the truth. Scholars today are writing more about Camille's contributions to Rodin's success and how he plagiarized her work. Camille even has her own museum now. The Claudel Museum opened in 2017 in the French town of Nogent-sur-Seine, where Camille made her very first sculpture as a little girl. The public can now see clearly why Rodin tried so desperately to destroy her.

Learn More

Young, Arnesia. "Camille Claudel: The Tumultuous Life and Incredible Work of a French Sculptor." *My Modern Met* (blog), January 8, 2021. https://mymodernnet.com/camille-claudel/.

13

SHE DISCOVERED DNA, THEN THREE MEN STOLE HER WORK AND WON THE NOBEL PRIZE

Some scientific thefts are hard to prove, but this one is easy. Rosalind Franklin discovered DNA's structure by using a highly specialized X-ray camera to capture its image in a photograph. Her colleague then stole the photo and shared it with two male scientists at a different lab. Those three men then published Rosalind's work as their own and won a Nobel Prize for "discovering" DNA. Rosalind didn't complain because she didn't know her work had been stolen. The truth wouldn't come until many years after her death.

Rosalind Franklin was born in England on July 25, 1920, the second of five children in an affluent Jewish family. Her father, Ellis Arthur Franklin, was a London banker who taught at a working men's college; her mother was a homemaker. Rosalind's family often took in Jews who were being exiled from Hitler's Germany.

At age six, Rosalind went to St. Paul's School for Girls, a private day school. She excelled in math and science and graduated high school at age eleven. She then went to one of the only colleges for girls in London that taught physics and chemistry. She earned a bachelor's degree in 1938 and won

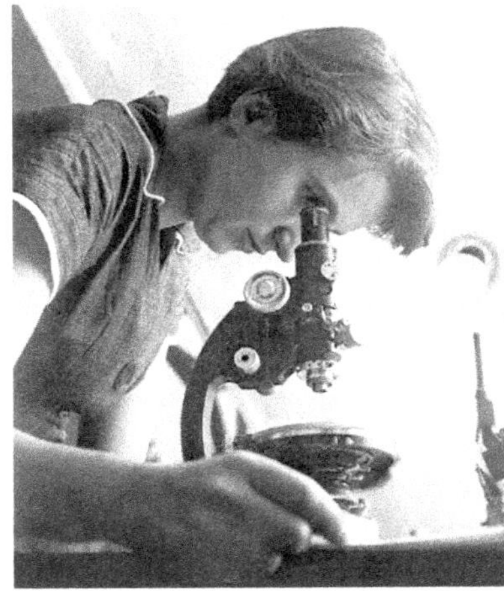

Rosalind Franklin in her lab at King's College London, 1955. Courtesy MRC Laboratory of Molecular Biology. Reproduced under a Creative Commons Attribution-Share Alike 4.0 International license, https://creativecommons.org/licenses/by-sa/4.0/deed.en.

a scholarship to study physics and chemistry at Newnham College at the University of Cambridge.

Rosalind also worked in a lab at Cambridge, where she learned how to photograph atoms using X-ray technology and crystallography. Crystallography shoots invisible rays at atoms that bounce off or diffract onto film. The diffraction process produces a pattern that can be translated into a three-dimensional image using mathematical calculations. Rosalind's supervisor at the time, Ronald George Wreyford Norish, would later win a Nobel Prize in Chemistry. Rosalind published five academic papers while studying at Cambridge and was awarded her PhD in 1945 in molecular biology and crystallography.

Rosalind next worked at one of the best labs in Paris, where she perfected her technique as an expert in X-ray diffraction photography. In 1951 she accepted a more prestigious position at King's College London, where there was an X-ray diffraction unit. A male scientist at the lab named Morris Wilkins had obtained early images of DNA, but they were not clear enough to reveal its structure.

When Rosalind arrived at King's College London, Wilkins was on vacation, so the lab's director, J. T. Randall, put Rosalind in charge and assigned Wilkins's PhD student

Raymond Gosling to work under Rosalind's supervision. The lab was in poor shape, so Rosalind initially focused on improving its functionality and acquiring better equipment. By the time Wilkins returned from vacation, Rosalind was the boss. Wilkins was not pleased.

Few women worked in the lab, and those who did were not welcome to eat or socialize with men. Wilkins treated Rosalind with hostility; Rosalind ignored him and focused on her research.

Meanwhile, an American scientist named James Watson was planning a move to London because he had attended a conference in Naples, Italy, where Wilkins showed one of his early photos of DNA. Watson wanted to work with Wilkins, but Wilkins wasn't interested, so he took a position at the University of Cambridge and worked under the direction of Nobel laureate Sir William Lawrence Bragg at the school's Cavendish Laboratory. While there, Watson teamed up with British scientist Francis Crick, and the two men set out to discover DNA's structure.

Rosalind was already making great progress in her lab and was the first to capture images showing two distinct forms of DNA. Scientists knew there were two forms of DNA, but they had never been photographed separately. Mixed together, they were indistinguishable, but Rosalind was able to capture their images separately.

Because Rosalind could now see the two different forms of DNA, she was able to focus her work on getting clearer images of each type. Her first images were not very clear, but she invited other scientists to a presentation where she discussed her findings. Watson sent Crick to listen, and a week later, relying on Rosalind's presentation, the men built what they believed was a physical model of DNA's structure. They invited a group of scientists, including Rosalind, to view their work.

Rosalind immediately knew that their structure was wrong. She explained to the audience why it was obviously incorrect, which embarrassed Watson and Crick. Their lab director forbade Watson and Crick to continue their research.

Rosalind fine-tuned her work and, in 1952, finally obtained a clear photograph of DNA's signature X structure. Famously

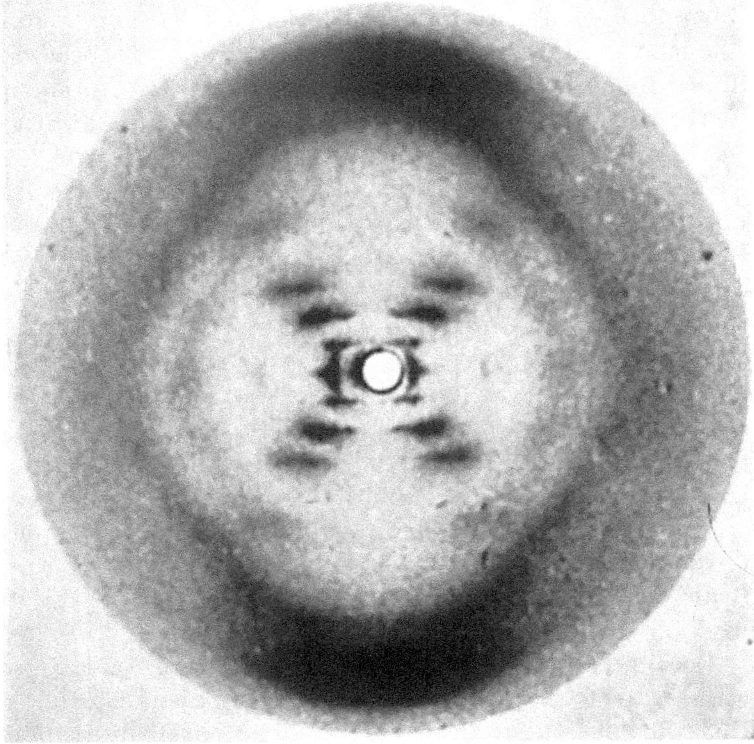

Photo 51. Courtesy Sadegh Mirshamsi. Reproduced under a Creative Commons Attribution-Share Alike 4.0 International license, https://creativecommons.org/licenses/by-sa/4.0/deed.en.

known as Photo 51, it revealed never-before-seen images of DNA's double helix. By this time, Rosalind was making plans to leave King's College London, but she agreed to stay long enough to interpret and mathematically explain how Photo 51 reveals DNA's structure. It had taken a hundred hours to capture the image; it would take months to do the calculations necessary to show exactly what DNA's double helix looked like. Until then, she would not share her photo with other scientists.

While Rosalind got busy on her calculations, Watson and Crick kept building models based on speculation and guesswork. Forbidden to work on DNA at their own lab, they teamed up with another scientist, Peter Pauling, son of acclaimed Nobel Prize–winning chemist Linus Pauling. Pauling helped Watson and Crick build models, but they were consistently incorrect.

Watson knew he could build the correct model if he had access to Rosalind's work, so he went to visit her at King's College and asked if she would share her data with him. Rosalind said no, but when Watson left her office, he ran into Wilkins, who secretly showed him Photo 51. Watson knew that this was the definitive photo he needed to produce a model of DNA's structure. He sketched a copy of the photo before he left. Watson would also need Rosalind's observational data to interpret the photo correctly. He got those data from a colleague at Cambridge who inappropriately gave him one of Rosalind's informal reports.

Watson and Crick told their lab director about Photo 51 and got permission to start building DNA models again. Rosalind, in the meantime, had completed her calculations and had mathematical proof of DNA's structure. She began writing a paper to explain her findings, but before she could submit it for publication, Watson and Crick invited her to examine their latest DNA model. Rosalind knew instantly it was correct because she had finished her calculations, but she had no idea they had created their model based on her stolen work. So convinced was Rosalind that Watson and Crick had figured out DNA's structure on their own that she added a note to her paper giving them credit for the discovery and saying that her work had confirmed their work.

Watson and Crick quickly began writing a paper about their "discovery" and planned to submit it to the journal *Nature,* but they knew the editors would ask to see their calculations, and they had nothing to show. Their lab director had no choice but to reach out to the director of Rosalind's lab and suggest that they publish Watson and Crick's paper simultaneously with Rosalind's, as this was the only way to give the editors underlying scientific support for Watson and Crick's model. *Nature* published both papers in the same edition in 1953 but put Rosalind's paper second, implying that her discovery had come after Watson and Crick's.

By this time, Rosalind had left King's College for Birkbeck College at the University of London. She headed the virus research lab there from 1953 to 1958 and made numerous discoveries about the complex nature of viruses. In five years she published seventeen papers. Her work was foundational to scientists' understanding of how viruses function and cause disease. The man with whom she collaborated on this important work, Aaron Klug, would later win a Nobel Prize.

Rosalind visited the United States in 1956 and returned to England with severe abdominal pain. She was diagnosed with ovarian cancer, caused by exposure to radiation from the X-ray technology she used in her work. Rosalind continued her research until just weeks before her death in 1958 at age thirty-seven. She never found out that Wilkins had secretly shown Photo 51 to Watson. In 1962 Watson, Crick, and Wilkins won the Nobel Prize for discovering the structure of DNA. They made no mention of Rosalind at the award ceremony.

In 1968 Watson published a book titled *The Double Helix,* in which he explained how he "discovered" DNA's structure. Knowing that Rosalind was deceased, he described her variously as unattractive, uncooperative, and incompetent at interpreting X-ray data. He confessed to using Rosalind's work without her knowledge or permission and even admitted that he could not have built his model without her data. Watson later became head of the National Center for Human Genome Research, now the National Human Genome Research Institute, at the National Institutes of Health before being appointed chancellor at the prestigious Cold Spring Harbor Laboratory of Quantitative Biology in New York. Cold Spring subsequently severed ties with Watson after he made sexist comments about women in science and racist comments about the intelligence of Black people. A follow-up book published in 1975, titled *Rosalind Franklin and DNA,* revealed in detail how Watson, Crick, and Wilkins stole Rosalind's work.

Thanks to the many scientists who have spoken up for Rosalind, she is finally getting the credit she deserves. The Rosalind Franklin Institute was recently founded in her honor, and in 2004 the Chicago Hospital–College of Medicine

Rosalind Franklin University of Medicine and Science, Chicago, Illinois. Courtesy Ancheta Wis. Reproduced under a Creative Commons Attribution-ShareAlike 3.0 Unported license, https://creativecommons.org/licenses/by-sa/3.0.

was renamed the Rosalind Franklin University of Medicine and Science. These things are helpful, as are the numerous awards and accolades that have been bestowed upon Rosalind since her death in 1958, but the Nobel Committee has yet to dethrone the thieves who took credit for Rosalind's work.

Learn More

Maddox, Brenda. *Rosalind Franklin: The Dark Lady of DNA*. New York: HarperCollins, 2002.

Sayre, Anne. *Rosalind Franklin and DNA*. New York: W. W. Norton, 1975.

14

A WOMAN DESIGNED WINDSHIELD WIPERS, BUT NOBODY CARED UNTIL A MAN REDESIGNED THEM

It's hard to imagine driving a car in the rain or snow without windshield wipers. Even a little bit of rain makes driving dangerous, never mind when things get torrential, but not that long ago, cars didn't have wipers at all. In fact, when automobiles were first manufactured in the United States in the late 1800s, they were essentially motorized buggies with big wheels and no windows.

Before automobile manufacturers began mass-producing cars with windshields, streetcars and trollies transported lots of people, especially in big cities. Some had windshields in the front to protect riders and drivers from the weather. While riding in a New York City streetcar one snowy day in 1902, a woman named Mary Anderson noticed the driver struggling to wipe snow off the windshield with his arm. She came up with an idea for a device that could be attached to the windshield and operated from inside to wipe away rain and snow. Mary got a patent for her invention in 1903 and tried to sell it to automobile manufacturers, but they weren't interested. Nobody paid attention to her invention until many years later, when a man copied Mary's idea and

Mary Anderson, circa 1910.

got his own patent, and then another man tweaked it and sued automobile manufacturers for using "his" invention without paying him.

Mary Anderson was born in rural Alabama on February 19, 1866, to John and Rebecca Anderson. Mary moved with her mother and sister to Birmingham after her father died when she was only four. She moved to California in her mid-twenties, where she ran a cattle ranch and vineyard before returning to Alabama in 1898 to care for an ailing aunt. After her aunt died in 1902, Mary took a trip to New York.

Mary loved New York and often traveled by streetcar. One fateful snowy day, Mary noticed the driver reaching his arm outside to wipe snow off the windshield. Watching the man struggle inspired Mary's idea for a device that could clear the windshield, and she hired a designer to sketch her design. Then she went to a local machine company to produce a prototype. When it was done, Mary applied for a patent for what she called a "window cleaning device" for vehicles that can "remove snow, ice, or sleet from the window." On November 10, 1903, she was awarded a patent.

Mary's invention had a lever on the inside that a driver could control, which would manipulate a rubber blade on the outside. It was spring-loaded to make the blade move back and forth, and it had a counterweight to keep the blade in contact with the window. Unlike today's windshield wipers, Mary's invention could be removed when not needed.

Automobiles were not yet popular in 1903, though that had begun to change in August 1902, when Theodore Roosevelt became the first US president to ride in a car. Mary tried to sell her patent to automobile manufacturers, but they declined, claiming that they did not see its commercial value. Some even criticized Mary's invention as a possible hazard to drivers because they would be distracted by the wipers' movement.

Windshield wipers may not have seemed important in 1902, as barely any cars were on the road. The Olds Motor Vehicle Company (now Oldsmobile) had just begun manufacturing them in an assembly-line system, producing only 425 in the first year. The Buick and Ford Motor Companies followed in 1903, and Ford sold its first personal-use car that same year to a dentist for $850—at a time when the average

Streetcar with no wipers on its front windows, Washington, DC, circa 1890. Photograph by the National Photo Company.

annual salary for a manufacturing job was only $541; dentists earned around $1,100. By the end of 1903, the United States had eighty car manufacturers that produced 325 different vehicles, though the popular Model T Ford wouldn't be invented for another five years.

Ford manufactured seventeen hundred cars in 1904, but they were still only a curiosity, and many people found them offensive, often yelling "get a horse" when they saw someone driving one. Advertisements urged people to buy cars because, unlike horses, they could be left out in the rain or cold without the owner feeling bad.

In 1905, as more people began buying cars, Mary again tried to sell her patent, this time to the Canadian company Dinning and Eckenstein, which specialized in the sale of patents for a commission. They declined, saying, "We regret to state we do not consider it to be of such commercial value as would warrant our undertaking its sale." They weren't wrong; manufacturers were still not installing windshield wipers on new cars.

As late as 1913, when the automobile industry was booming and consumer demand was high, windshield wipers were not routinely being installed. In 1916 they finally became standard equipment, but manufacturers did not credit or pay Mary for her invention, even though her patent was still active.

In 1919 a man named William Folberth invented an automatic version of Mary's design. It had two speeds, fast and slow. Many years later, a man named Robert Kearns designed a similar device that could move at an intermediate pace. Kearns claimed that his design was less distracting to drivers.

Kearns got a patent in 1967 and, like Mary, tried to sell it, but the three biggest car manufacturers, General Motors, Ford, and Chrysler, declined. Kearns was furious when Ford and Chrysler then started installing his intermediate-speed wipers in their cars, so he sued them for patent infringement. He first sued Ford in 1978. Ford knew that Kearns was not the original inventor because it knew about Mary's and Folberth's patents. Ford claimed that Kearns didn't deserve compensation because all he did was take advantage of other people's inventions. Unfortunately for Ford, the law was clear that a

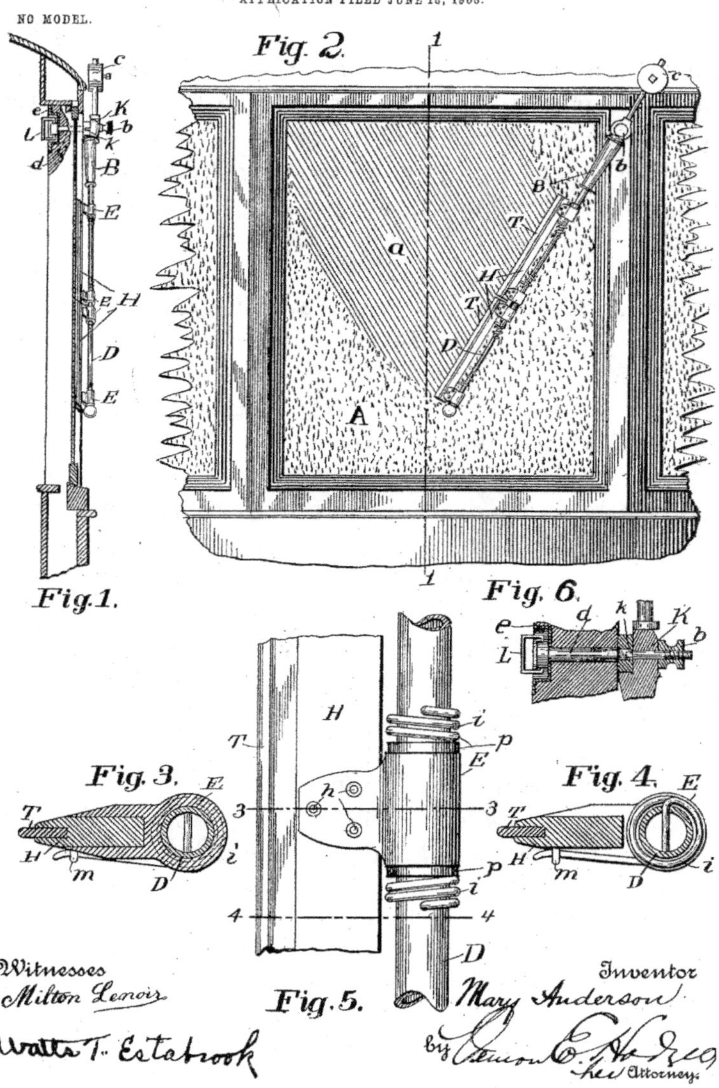

Mary Anderson's patent drawing for her "window cleaning device." Patent 743801, 1903. Courtesy US Patent Office.

person can be granted a patent for a new way of using an existing object or when an invention uses "former elements in a new assemblage."

Kearns won his lawsuit against Ford in 1990 and was awarded $10 million. He had also sued Chrysler in 1982 and, in 1995, won another $30 million. In total, Kearns filed more than a dozen lawsuits against car dealers and manufacturers, though not all were successful.

Kearns's high-profile victories in court earned him a little justice and a lot of money, but they also misled the public to believe that he was the original inventor of the windshield wiper. Kearns himself never made such a claim, as he knew his design was only a modification of an existing invention. The true inventor was Mary—she was the one who conceived the original idea that others modified; she was the one with the creative mind who saw a problem that needed fixing and came up with a solution. But Mary was a woman, with only limited rights. All the men who dismissed Mary's invention as worthless knew they could disrespect her without legal consequence.

Mary died in 1953 at age eighty-seven. She had no children of her own, but she had nieces and great-nieces and great-great-nieces, and she was an inspiration to them all. Her great-great-niece Sara-Scott Wingo, speaking to National Public Radio in 2017, said she suspected that Mary never got the credit she deserved because she was an independent woman—she didn't have a father or a husband or a son, and "the world was kind of run by men back then." Wingo's three daughters still talk about Mary "a lot," and they remind themselves to "be open and receptive to . . . [their] own Mary Anderson moments." No doubt they were standing proud when Mary was inducted into the National Inventors Hall of Fame in 2011.

Learn More

"Mary Anderson: The Unheralded Inventor of the Windshield Wiper." *National Inventors Hall of Fame Blog,* n.d. https://www.invent.org/blog/inventors/mary-anderson-windshield-wipers.

15

FRANK LLOYD WRIGHT CLAIMED HER DESIGNS AS HIS OWN

Frank Lloyd Wright's building designs are renowned for the way they blend into the environment and evoke a sense of balance between man and nature. Less well known is that Wright did a whole lot wrong by one of his employees, a woman named Marion Mahony Griffin. Marion worked for Wright for many years and produced countless architectural drawings and paintings, but most of her work was credited to Wright—at his insistence.

Marion Mahony was born in Chicago, Illinois, on February 14, 1871, the youngest of five children. Her father, Jeremiah, was a journalist, poet, and teacher. Her mother, Clara, was a teacher. Right after Mary was born, they moved to the rural Illinois town of Winnetka. The Great Chicago Fire of 1871 had killed hundreds of people and destroyed thousands of buildings. Mary's parents wanted to escape the devastation and raise their children in a more peaceful environment.

Life was quiet in bucolic Winnetka, but in 1881 the family house burned down. Marion's father died soon after that, when Marion was only eleven. Marion's grandparents, who had been friendly with Abraham Lincoln, helped to raise her.

Marion Mahony Griffin shortly after graduating from MIT.

As a young girl, Marion loved nature. She noticed the loss of natural space as more and more people left Chicago and started building homes in the suburbs and outlying areas. She spent a lot of time outdoors and would later describe the natural world as the "greatest of teachers," especially for children. As an adult, Marion worried about the impact of growing populations on the environment. She referred to Hubbard Woods, her childhood home in Winnetka, as "God's university."

Marion was inspired by her cousin Dwight Perkins to study architecture and design. Perkins had graduated from the Massachusetts Institute of Technology's (MIT's) School of Architecture, and he encouraged Marion to apply. She was accepted in 1890 and graduated with a bachelor's degree in 1894—only the second woman to do so. The first woman, Sophia Hayden, graduated with the same degree four years earlier in 1890 but, as a woman, was unable to find work as an architect, even after winning a prestigious design contest in 1893. She became a mechanical drawing teacher at a Boston high school.

Marion had better luck. When she returned to Chicago after graduation, she worked for her cousin and was the first female to be licensed as an architect in Illinois. Her cousin's firm was located at Steinway Hall, where other architects, including Frank Lloyd Wright, had their offices. Marion took

Marion's design for the K. C. DeRhodes House, South Bend, Indiana, showing her initials, MLM, in the foreground in the form of a spider, 1906. Perspective. Ink, pencil, and colored pencil on paper, 18 1/2 × 25 3/4 in.

a job with Wright in 1895 as his first employee. She designed buildings, furniture, stained glass windows, and decorative wall panels.

Marion's love for the environment was evident in her beautiful artistic renderings of buildings because she surrounded them with trees and landscapes. Although Wright was talented, his drawings were more geometric, whereas Marion's were usually of buildings with clean lines, surrounded by the pastoral softness of nature.

Wright insisted that all the work done by architects in his firm be credited only to him. As a result, Marion's unique style soon became known as Frank Lloyd Wright's style. In 1898 he moved his office from Steinway Hall to his expanded home office, which he had redesigned to have two different entrances—one for his family and one for his business clients. Interestingly, Marion's final thesis assignment at MIT was to design a home where an artist could live and run a business.

Wright taking credit for Marion's work did not sit well with Marion. In one 1906 drawing she added a bird and a small spider to the bottom left foreground. The spider was made using Marion's initials, MLM, in an obvious attempt to reveal that she, and not Wright, had created the design. When Wright noticed what Marion had done, he took a pen and wrote on the bottom right side of the picture, "designed by Mahony," along with a notation that she had been inspired by Japanese architecture. This was likely Wright's way of making clear to Marion that he would notice if she again tried to give herself credit. It may also have been Wright's way of creating the public impression that none of Wright's work should have been attributed to Marion unless it included a notation by him giving Marion credit.

Marion was associated with Wright's studio for almost fifteen years, during which time she contributed more than half the drawings to Wright's famous Wasmuth Portfolio—a book containing one hundred lithographs of building plans and architectural designs from 1893 to 1909. Other than the one 1906 drawing to which Marion added her initials, none of Marion's drawings were attributed to her. Experts who later learned the truth have since described Marion as the "greatest architectural delineator of her generation."

Even Wright's son John Lloyd Wright credited Marion with making valuable contributions to Wright's reputation as a leader of the Prairie Style of architecture. The Prairie Style grew out of a desire of midwesterners to find a building style of their own, rather than copying the designs of East Coast homes, which they saw as borrowed from Europe and thus not uniquely American. Midwestern architects wanted something original, more in keeping with the land-loving American spirit. Wright took credit for conceiving the Prairie Style, but in fact it was writer and architect Louis Sullivan who called for an original American design rooted in nature and based on simple lines that emphasized vertical space rather than height. Marion famously said that Wright's habit of taking credit for the Prairie Style movement caused the movement's early death in the United States.

A bust of Marion Mahony Griffin overlooking Canberra, Australia—the city she mostly designed, though only her husband's name appeared on the design documents. Used with permission.

Wright was married when Marion first started working for him, but he left his wife and children for the wife of a client and eloped to Europe in 1909, leaving his studio and a lot of unfinished work behind. He offered his projects and clients to Marion, but she declined and instead began working with Hermann von Holst, who had taken on some of Wright's unfinished commissions. Marion made clear to von Holst that she alone would maintain control of her designs and would be given sole credit for all her work. She became the lead architect on several well-known projects in Michigan that Wright had abandoned, including the famous Amberg House and Henry Ford's Michigan mansion Fair Lane.

Now working for von Holst, Marion returned to Steinway Hall, where she met an architect twelve years her junior named Walter Griffin, who had also worked for Wright. They soon married and began working together in 1911. Marion designed her own buildings and painted watercolor renderings of Walter's designs. Together, the couple entered an international contest, commissioned by the Australian government, to design a series of buildings for the new capital city of Canberra—at the time a virtual wasteland.

Government officials wanted the buildings to reflect the country's idealistic commitment to democracy. Marion and Walter won the competition in 1912 and, in 1914, moved to Australia to oversee the project's development. Walter would later say that it was Marion who did nearly all the designs and drawings for Canberra.

When the couple arrived in Australia, Marion was legally prohibited from practicing architecture on her own because she was a woman, so she worked for Walter. She also spent more time on her art, especially paintings on silk. The couple settled in Sydney in the 1920s, but Walter moved to India in 1935 when he was asked to design a library for the University of Lucknow. While there, he was commissioned to do even more design work, so Marion joined him in 1936 and helped oversee the construction of several projects.

Less than a year later, Walter died of peritonitis, and Marion returned to Australia. Before long, she moved back to Chicago. By then in her late sixties, she was mostly retired from architecture and design work. During her retirement, Marion spent years organizing a compilation of her work and writing a memoir more than fourteen hundred pages long, with 650 illustrations, titled *The Magic of America* (1949).

Meanwhile, Frank Lloyd Wright returned to the United States and moved to California in 1957, after he was hired to design the Marin County Civic Center in San Rafael. Wright died in 1959, before the Civic Center was built, so his protégé, Aaron Green, oversaw the project. Many thought the building was a strange choice for the area because Wright said his philosophy was to design buildings that blend in with their environment, and the Civic Center did not reflect the San Francisco Bay area. It had lots of arches and was decorated with gold columns, railings, and balls. The motifs were Arabian, and many of the walls were pink stucco. It later came out that the building had originally been designed for a Saudi Arabian client of Wright's, but when the contract was canceled, he submitted the same plans for the Marin County project.

Marion died soon after Wright, in 1961; she was ninety and penniless. Many of the homes she designed have multimillion-dollar price tags today.

Learn More

Griffin, Marion Mahony. *The Magic of America*. 1949; reprint, Chicago: Art Institute of Chicago, 2007.

Korporaal, Glenda. *Making Magic: The Marion Mahony Griffin Story*. Toronto: BookPOD, 2015.

16

VICTOR MILLS SAYS HE INVENTED DISPOSABLE DIAPERS, BUT THAT'S POOP

Disposable diapers liberated women almost as much as the right to vote did. The freedom to change a smelly diaper and toss it away rather than having to be near laundry every time a little darling pooped untethered moms from the home, so it should come as no surprise that a mom came up with the idea. But a man claimed the invention as his own.

Marion O'Brien was born in South Bend, Indiana, on October 15, 1917. Her mother passed away when she was seven, so she was raised by her father, Miles, who ran a manufacturing plant with his twin brother. Miles was also an inventor whose designs include the South Bend lathe, which is a special tool used to make automobile gears and gun barrels.

As a child, Marion spent a lot of time at her father's factory, where she saw firsthand how her father's inventions helped solve problems and improve his business. Inspired, Marion came up with an idea for a new tooth cleaning powder while still in elementary school.

Marion attended Rosemont College in Pennsylvania and graduated in 1939 with a bachelor's degree in English. She worked in New York as an editor at *Vogue* before marrying a leather importer named James Donovan in 1942. She then

June 12, 1951 M. DONOVAN 2,556,800

DIAPER WRAP

Filed Jan. 19, 1949

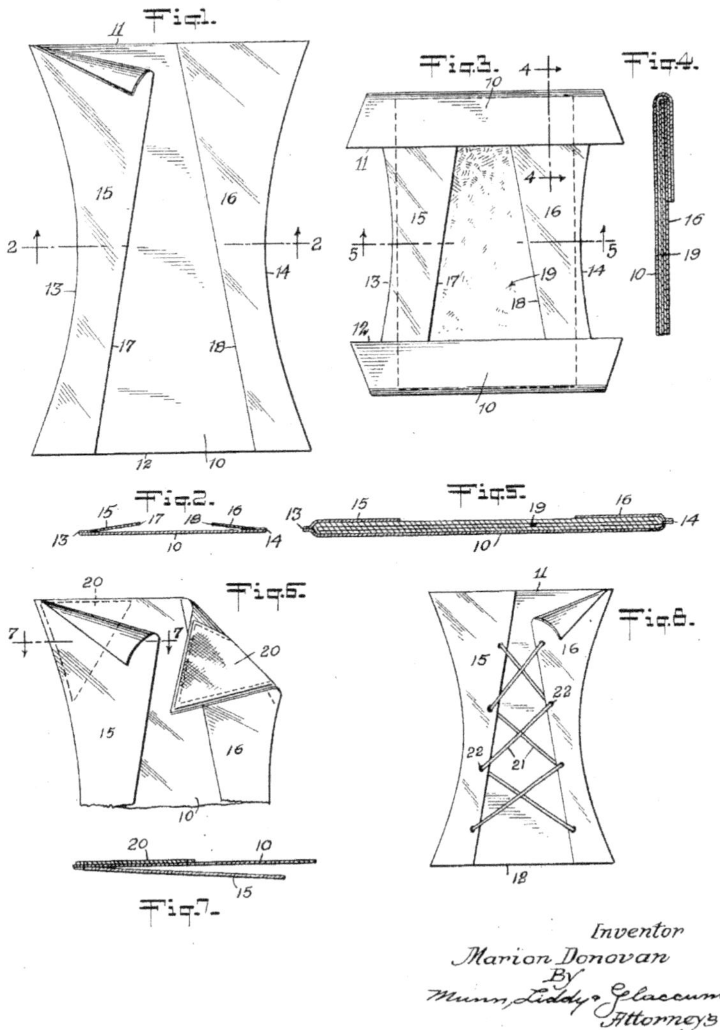

Marion O'Brien Donovan's patent drawing for her "Boater." Patent 2556800, 1951. Courtesy US Patent Office.

resigned from *Vogue* and moved to Connecticut to start a family.

Marion eventually had three children, and her inventive mind went to work on ideas to make life at home easier. When her second child was an infant, she was overwhelmed by the burden of cloth diapers because they were not water resistant. Her babies would soil their diapers, their clothing, and whatever they were lying on. This created lots of laundry and required the changing of bed linens, often in the middle of the night when Marion was exhausted. Cloth diapers also caused diaper rash, making babies miserable.

It was hard to predict when a baby might soak through a diaper, so moms couldn't be away from home for long periods without having a plan for how to deal with a diaper change. Marion thought all these problems would be solved if she could somehow cover the diaper with waterproof material.

The first thing she tried was a shower curtain. She took down the one that was hanging in her bathroom and cut it into diaper-sized pieces. She doubled the layers and made an opening so a cloth diaper could be inserted inside of it. This would protect clothing and bed linens and keep wetness away from her baby's skin. Better yet, it could be used over and over again.

Rubber diaper covers already existed, but the material was not breathable, and it only protected the outside of the diaper. Parents didn't like them because they did nothing for diaper rash and pinched babies' skin. After experimenting with her shower curtain, Marion decided to make diaper covers out of nylon parachute cloth because the fabric was breathable and waterproof. She used snaps instead of diaper pins, because they worked better with the material, and called her invention the Boater because it "looked like a boat" and "helped babies stay afloat."

Marion tried to sell her idea to companies that made baby products but couldn't find a buyer, so she manufactured it herself. When she debuted the Boater at Saks Fifth Avenue in New York City in 1949, it was an instant success. She received four patents for the Boater in 1951 and sold it that year to the Keko Corporation for $1 million ($10 million in today's money).

More affection for and from baby
with revolutionary

Boater

new. NYLON diaper cover

Now you can be sure of ABSOLUTELY DRY bundling clothes and bedding with this amazing BOATER. Brilliantly fashioned to give comfort to baby—bind-proof, leak-proof, it has plenty of freedom for action. Fold disposable or regular diapers into its waterproofed NYLON pocket and snap on. Takes a few minutes to launder. Designed with *four* protection flaps that keep all baby's clothes *as dry as hospital cotton.*

Three adjustable snaps on all sizes—small, medium, large, extra large. In pink, blue, white, yellow; at $1.95*

*Fair Traded

Advertisement for the Boater. Marion O'Brien Donovan Papers, Archives Center, National Museum of American History, Smithsonian Institution.

Despite her success, some in the media were condescending, describing her as "the inventing housewife." One reporter even wrote, "Marion Donovan . . . knows nothing about science. . . . She is baffled by any mechanism more intricate than an eggbeater." They could not have been more wrong.

Because the Boater was so popular, Marion knew there was a market for an entirely disposable diaper that could be thrown away after each use. She experimented with different materials and made samples in her house. Her daughter Christine recalls that "every room in the house was a laboratory" and that the children "formed an assembly line to work on prototypes." Marion eventually used a moisture-wicking paper material and covered it in waterproof nylon. She brought a sample to all the major paper companies to try to sell it, but they said it was unnecessary and impractical. They told her women had no desire to use disposable diapers, as they were perfectly content with washable cloth diapers.

Marion was disheartened but, unlike with the Boater, took no steps to manufacture disposable diapers on her own. Instead, she enrolled at Yale University and, in 1958, received a master's degree in architecture. She was one of only three women in her graduating class.

Years later, several companies began mass-producing disposable diapers, but none of them credited Marion. The first was Procter and Gamble, which boasted that the idea for disposable diapers came from one of its employees—a man named Victor Mills.

Mills had no interest in diapers until after Procter and Gamble bought the Charmin Paper Company in 1957. As a Procter and Gamble employee, Mills focused on soap and cake mixes, but after Procter and Gamble acquired the Charmin Paper Company, he was asked to come up with new ideas for paper products.

Mills says he conceived the idea for disposable diapers because he changed his grandchildren's cloth diapers and thought disposable diapers would be less messy. He was correct about the messy part, but did he really conceive the idea for disposable diapers based on his experience as a diaper-changing grandfather? How many white-collar corporate executives in 1957 changed their grandchildren's diapers?

Mills used a drink-and-wet doll as a baby model to experiment with different types of paper and liners and eventually came up with a product called Pampers. The original Pampers diaper was rectangular and had a rayon liner. The liner was stacked with layers of tissue and covered with plastic. It was held together with pins, and the edges were pleated to fit around babies' legs. Mills had essentially "invented" the same disposable diaper that Marion had tried to sell to paper companies years earlier.

Regardless of Mills's story, he can hardly be credited with inventing disposable diapers. Marion's leak-proof diaper cover was indisputably invented long before Pampers were created and was the inspiration behind Marion's design for an entirely disposable diaper. Disposable diapers were also on the market in Europe well before Procter and Gamble bought the Charmin Paper Company. Nonetheless, when Mills died in November 1997, his obituary in the *New York Times* (a newspaper that should have known better, given the widely publicized success of Marion's Boater at Saks Fifth Avenue in 1949) described him as the "father of disposable diapers."

Procter and Gamble deserves credit for eventually developing a more absorbent diaper that used polymers to hold moisture without getting heavy, and it came up with a new way of keeping disposable diapers together using tape or Velcro-like material rather than pins or snaps. But the original idea for disposable diapers did not come from the brain of a grandfather who didn't like changing cloth diapers; it came from the inventive mind of a young mother from Indiana who conceived the idea for the same reason other people come up with good ideas: because it made her life easier.

Marion invented many other products and registered twenty patents between 1951 and 1996. Several of her ideas made life easier for women, such as a thirty-garment compact hanger, a soap dish that drained into the sink, and an elastic cord that connected over the shoulder so a woman could zip up the back of her dress.

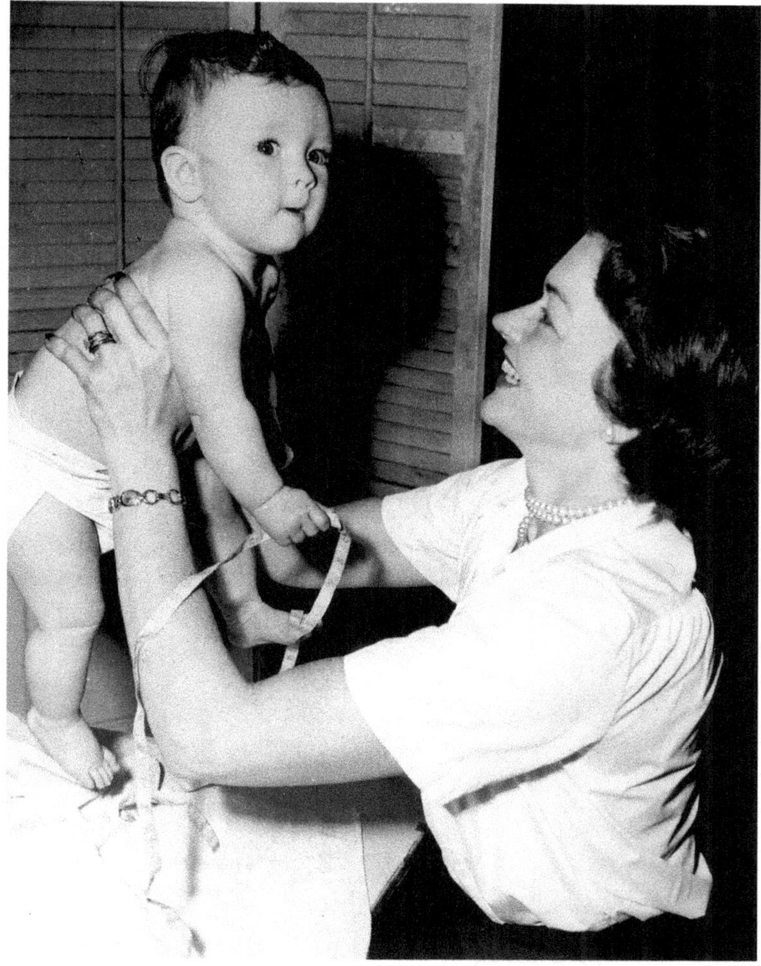

Marion holding a baby wearing the Boater. Marion O'Brien Donovan Papers, Archives Center, National Museum of American History, Smithsonian Institution.

Marion died in New York on November 4, 1998, at age eighty-one. She never got the credit she deserved for inventing the disposable diaper, but all these years later, she's getting a little help from the guys on late-night TV. Trevor Noah aired Marion's story on *The Daily Show* in 2018.

Learn More

Lemelson–MIT. "Marion Donovan, Disposable Diaper." n.d. https://lemelson.mit.edu/resources/marion-donovan.

17

SHE WAS MORE THAN F. SCOTT'S WIFE

Acclaimed essayist and novelist F. Scott Fitzgerald has been described as one of America's greatest writers. He is often listed among the best novelists of all time, while his wife, Zelda, is barely known at all. Yet F. Scott used her writings in his work, including in his most famous book, *The Great Gatsby* (1925), without attribution.

Zelda Sayre was born the youngest of six children in Alabama on July 24, 1900. Her parents were wealthy, and she was a bit of a spoiled brat. Her father was a justice of the Alabama Supreme Court, descended from early settlers of New York. Zelda also had relatives in the US Senate. Zelda was bright but uninterested in school. She spent much of her time socializing and refused to conduct herself in a "ladylike," southern manner.

Zelda met F. Scott Fitzgerald in 1918 while he was in the army, stationed in Alabama. The couple quickly fell in love and developed a relationship many have described as "intense" and "reckless." F. Scott boasted to Zelda about his plans to become a famous writer. He rewrote the first draft of a novel to make one of the lead characters seem more like Zelda, and Zelda gave him her personal diaries so he could make the character authentically resemble her personality.

Zelda Fitzgerald, 1919.

Zelda was a prolific writer herself. She kept a detailed journal of her daily life and wrote of her experiences in a style that has been compared to Emily Dickinson's.

By early 1919, the couple was engaged, though Zelda's family did not like F. Scott because he had no money and was a heavy drinker. Zelda agreed to marry him only after he published his first novel.

F. Scott's first novel, *This Side of Paradise,* was finally published in March 1920, and the couple were married in New York a few days later. Zelda and F. Scott were the "it" couple in Manhattan, often featured in society pages. It was the early-1900s Jazz Age, and people were always out on the town. The couple's active social life was marked by extreme alcohol abuse.

After too many scandalous headlines in New York, F. Scott and Zelda moved to Westport, Connecticut, where they lived for five months. Their time there, like their time in Manhattan, was marked by raucous socializing that provided many storylines for F. Scott's books.

In early 1921 Zelda became pregnant. She gave birth to a baby girl, Frances, in Minnesota, where F. Scott's family lived. She told F. Scott she hoped the baby would become a "beautiful fool," words he used years later in *The Great Gatsby*. Zelda was not especially interested in motherhood or domestic duties, so she hired servants to care for Frances and run the house. When she again became pregnant in 1922, she had an abortion.

Later that same year, F. Scott published *The Beautiful and the Damned,* and Zelda was asked by the *New York Tribune* to write a review. She was happy to oblige and pointed out in her piece that F. Scott had plagiarized her writings. "It seems to me that on one page I recognized a portion of an old diary of mine which mysteriously disappeared shortly after my marriage." She also wrote, "Mr. Fitzgerald . . . seems to believe that plagiarism begins at home." Zelda was light-hearted in her piece, but she resented F. Scott's use of her words without attribution.

Zelda's critique of F. Scott's book was well received, and she was asked to write for other publications. Over time she sold many short stories and articles and helped F. Scott write a play. The couple enjoyed success, but F. Scott was suffering from depression, and in 1924 they moved to Paris in the hope that his mood would improve.

F. Scott spent his time in Paris working on *The Great Gatsby* while Zelda became involved with another man. Zelda asked for a divorce, but F. Scott refused and locked her in their house. The couple remained married, but things were not going well.

F. Scott's first draft of *The Great Gatsby* left his editor unimpressed. Gatsby as a character had not been developed enough, so he asked F. Scott to edit the book to create a better sense of who he was and what he looked like. F. Scott turned to Zelda for help. She drew images of Gatsby that helped him create a more in-depth literary image.

Meanwhile, George Nathan, F. Scott's editor, asked Zelda if he could publish her diaries because by then Zelda was a well-known cultural icon. Zelda loved the idea, but F. Scott objected. He had already used some of her writings in previous novels and did not want the public to find out that he had claimed Zelda's words as his own. He also planned to use more of Zelda's writings in future books, so he took Zelda's

Cover of the first edition of Zelda's book, *Save Me the Waltz* (1932).

journals away from her and hid them. To this day, they have not been found.

The Great Gatsby was finished in fall 1924. Reviews were good, but it was a commercial failure. It would be many years before the book would earn its reputation as the "Great American Novel." The couple stayed together, but they were miserable. They traveled to Italy for vacation, where Zelda took up oil painting.

After returning to Paris, F. Scott met Ernest Hemingway, and the two became close friends, but Zelda did not like him and described him as a "phony." Hemingway in turn despised Zelda and told F. Scott she was crazy. Zelda was jealous of F. Scott's relationship with Ernest and suspected that they were having an affair.

By 1928 the couple had moved back to the United States and were living in Delaware. Zelda was bored; F. Scott became a severe alcoholic. In 1930 Zelda was sent to a mental hospital in France, where she was diagnosed with schizophrenia. She was later treated in Switzerland before being released in September 1931, after which she moved to Alabama with F. Scott because her father was dying. F. Scott later left Alabama for Hollywood in the hope of becoming a screenwriter. Zelda suffered a breakdown when her father died. She was admitted to a psychiatric facility at Johns Hopkins in 1932, where she wrote an entire novel in two months—a semiautobiographical account of her relationship with F. Scott. He was furious, not because Zelda exposed their private life, but because he was planning to use much of the same material in his next book. Zelda didn't care. She titled her book *Save Me the Waltz* and published it with F. Scott's publisher, Scribner Press, in late 1932. F. Scott's next novel, *Tender Is the Night,* was published by Scribner two years later.

Zelda eventually left Johns Hopkins but continued to struggle with mental illness, and in 1936 F. Scott had her institutionalized again, this time in North Carolina. He again went to California and began an affair with a Hollywood columnist but returned to North Carolina after getting in trouble for abusing her.

Public marker of the location in North Carolina where Zelda died. Courtesy North Carolina Highway Historical Marker Program. Used with permission.

When Zelda got out of the hospital, the couple took a trip to Cuba, but it was a disaster. F. Scott was beaten during a drunken brawl and checked himself into a mental hospital when they returned to the United States. Eventually, he went back to Hollywood. Zelda and F. Scott separated but stayed in touch. They had little money and no friends. F. Scott died in 1940 at age forty-four. Zelda moved in and out of psychiatric facilities before dying in 1948, at age forty-seven, when the hospital where she was living caught fire.

Zelda and F. Scott are buried together in Maryland, under a tombstone inscribed with the last words from *The Great Gatsby*: "So we beat on, boats against the current, borne back ceaselessly into the past."

The couple's lives became fodder for several books and movies, most of which are sympathetic to F. Scott and critical of Zelda as the source of his troubles. But during the women's movement, a writer named Nancy Milford published *Zelda: A Biography* (2011), in which she described Zelda as a talented artist who was abused and exploited by a wretched and controlling alcoholic husband. A similar biography, *The Subversive Art of Zelda Fitzgerald,* was penned in 2017 by Deborah Pike, who wrote that Zelda was a valuable contributor to women's art because she brought new perspectives to the lived experiences of women and the difficulties they endure at the hands of abusive male partners.

Scholars today are still intrigued by the fact that Zelda's book *Save Me the Waltz* and F. Scott's book *Tender Is the Night* tell the same story, but in dramatically different ways. They see the books as an important study in the different lenses through which men and women experience life.

New information about Zelda's life has raised questions about her role in F. Scott's work. Did an unhappy woman with mental health problems make her husband miserable and ruin his career, or did F. Scott self-destruct because he was paranoid that Zelda would expose him as a plagiarist? And where are Zelda's diaries?

Learn More

Milford, Nancy. *Zelda: A Biography.* New York: Harper Perennial, 2011.

Pike, Deborah. *The Subversive Art of Zelda Fitzgerald.* Columbia: University of Missouri Press, 2017.

Pike, Deborah. "Zelda Fitzgerald: A Creative Voice Curtailed Who Speaks to Our Cultural Moment." *The Conversation,* January 29, 2018. https://theconversation.com/Zelda-fitzgerald-a-creative-voice-curtailed-who-speaks-to-our-cultural-moment-90103.

18

A CURLING IRON IS NOT A HAIR STRAIGHTENER

Women today who like to flatten their curly locks can't imagine life without a hair straightener, but it wasn't until recently that they could buy one at the local drugstore.

Unsurprisingly, a woman came up with the idea for a hair straightener, though you wouldn't know it if you looked online for information. A search for articles about who invented the hair straightener brings up stories about two men, Isaac Shero and Marcel Grateau. Grateau was a hair stylist in France in the late 1800s who invented a curling iron that some used to try to flatten curls. Shero got a patent for a hair straightener in 1909, but it was issued nearly fifteen years after the same product was invented by a woman from Indiana named Ada Harris.

Ada Harris was born in Kentucky in 1870 and moved to Indiana as a child. When she graduated from high school, she became a teacher. She also spent a lot of time in hair salons, where women would gather not only for a hair wash but also to talk about their lives. It was in a hair salon in 1893 that Ada came up with the idea for a hair straightener. She saw how difficult it was for Black women to style and manage their hair. She wanted to invent a product to make things easier.

Ada Harris, date unknown.

Ada knew that the device had to be strong enough to press hair flat, and it had to be hot. Her design connected two long metal pieces together, each with a wide, flat plate at the end. The pieces were bound by a hinge that could squeeze the plates together. When hair was placed between the plates, it would flatten. There was no electricity in 1893, so the plates were heated by exposure to a flame or stove.

Ada hired a company to build a prototype, and on November 3, 1893, she filed a patent application for her invention. She wrote, "Be it known that I, ADA HARRIS, of Indianapolis, county of Marion, and state of Indiana, have invented a certain new and useful Hair-Straightener." She included a black-and-white drawing of a handheld item with two grips held together by a spring, each attached at the other end to a metal plate. She explained in her application that the purpose of her device was to "straighten curly hair and is especially of service to colored people in straightening their hair." Ada's invention included a comb piece that allowed the hair simultaneously to be pulled and smoothed flat. Her patent was granted on April 2, 1895.

In 1894 Ada traveled from her home in Indiana to the California Midwinter Exposition, an extension of the World's Fair tours that showcased new inventions. Ada brought her prototype and displayed it in a booth, hoping to find investors or maybe even to sell her patent to a company that specialized

(No Model.)

A. HARRIS.

HAIR STRAIGHTENER.

No. 536,802. Patented Apr. 2, 1895.

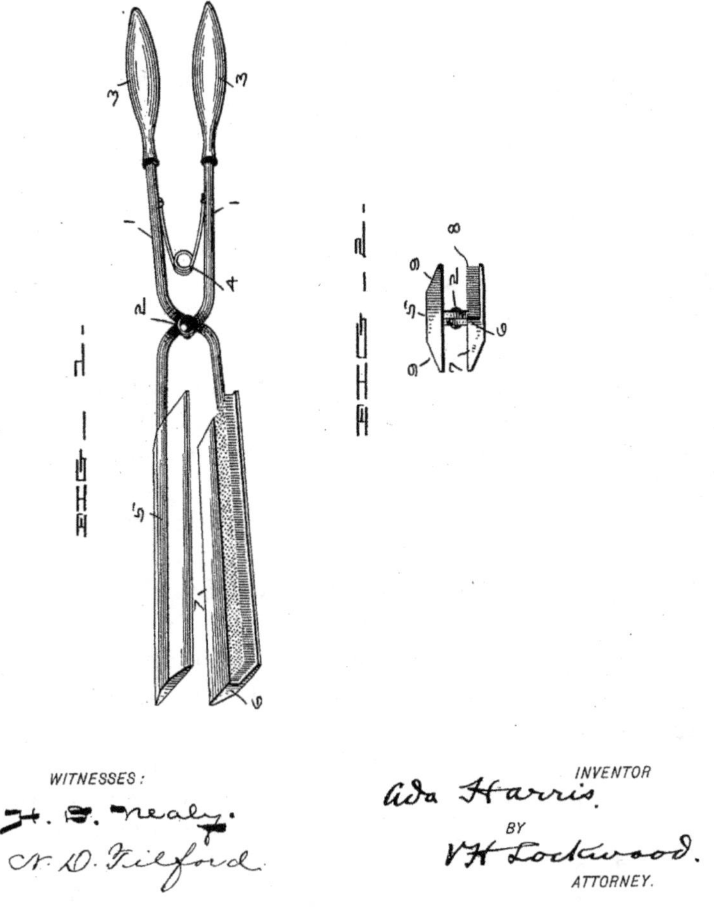

Ada Harris's patent drawing for her "hair straightener." Patent 536802, 1895. Courtesy US Patent Office.

in hair products, but there were no takers. Ada gave up and turned her attention to civic and social justice causes.

A few years later, Shero got busy stealing Ada's invention. On March 8, 1909, he filed a patent for a hair straightener, making only a slight change to Ada's design by removing the comb piece. Shero's application read, "Be it known that I, Isaac K. Shero, a citizen of the United States, residing at Okemah, in the county of Okfuskee and State of Oklahoma, have invented certain new and useful improvements in Hair-Straighteners of which the following is a specification. This invention relates to a novel device for application to the hair in order to straighten the same by the application of heat thereto. An object of this invention is to construct a device of this character which will do away with the necessity of providing a plurality of teeth for engagement with the hair which has a tendency to catch and break the same."

Shero conceded that he was copying Ada's patent, because he wrote that his design was an "improvement" of an existing design, as opposed to an original invention, and that the improvement was that his hair straightener did not have a comb piece. Removal of the comb may have justified the issuance of a new patent because the design was different than Ada's, but it did not make him the inventor of the hair straightener.

Shero's application was granted on December 14, 1909, only nine months after he applied for it. It took the Patent Office seventeen months—nearly twice as long—to grant Ada's patent, even though the Patent Office was much less busy in 1893, when she filed her application, because only half as many patents were issued that year compared to 1909. Was Ada's patent delayed because officials knew she was a Black woman? Her name made clear that she was a woman, and she mentioned that the invention would be helpful for "colored people." Shero, obviously male, made no mention of his design helping "colored people."

Once Shero got his patent, he began selling his invention and soon became known as the inventor of the hair straightener. Even today, the Wikipedia page for "hair iron" says nothing about Ada. Grateau is listed as the first person to use heated

Ada Harris in the *Indianapolis Star,* 1909.

metal to manipulate hair to become straight, and Shero is described as the person who actually invented and patented the hair straightener. Two women are mentioned too: a well-known hair salon owner named C. J. Walker who used hair straighteners in the early 1900s and a mentor of Walker's, Annie Malone, who invented a flattening comb. Ada isn't there at all.

Though never capitalizing on her invention, Ada was quite successful. She was a highly regarded leader in her community who donated her time to help people in need. She teamed up with two other women to start the Idle Hands Needles Club, which collected resources to provide fuel, food, and clothing for families. When Ada later moved to an impoverished area of Indiana, she worked as a teacher, established a boys' club, and raised money to help run a community grocery store. Ada also boldly rode a bicycle at a time when most women demurely declined, and she became a reporter for two Black newspapers. She even started a club at her church that later grew to three hundred members before it merged with the Indianapolis branch of the NAACP, one of the only branches that allowed Black women to serve in leadership roles. Ada served as a notary public and tireless advocate who helped Black women register to vote after the Nineteenth Amendment was adopted in 1920. She continued to teach and do community service throughout her life.

Ada died in 1927 without achieving wealth or fame for her invention, but it didn't bother her. She once told a reporter that her greatest ambition in life was for her race, "to see her people succeed." She wanted Black people "to have equal chance" and boasted not about her invention but that she had "spent [her] life for [her] race." As the *Indianapolis Star* said of Ada in 1909, she stayed busy "stirring ambition."

Ironically, fewer people today would know about all the good work Ada did as a humanitarian if she had not gained fame as yet another woman whose work was stolen by a man.

Learn More

Higgs, Catherine, Barbara A. Moss, and Earline Rae Ferguson, eds. *Stepping Forward: Black Women in Africa and the Americas.* Athens: Ohio University Press, 2002.

19

SHE DIED RIGHT AFTER INVENTING A TREATMENT FOR LEPROSY, THEN HER BOSS TOOK THE CREDIT

Imagine that you come up with a great idea for an invention and you're very excited because your boss thinks it's a great idea too. You get a prototype built and fill out your patent application, but before you have a chance to file it, something terrible happens, and you die. Now imagine that right after you die, your boss snatches up your invention and claims it as his own. That's exactly what happened to Alice Ball after she developed a treatment for leprosy.

Alice Augusta Ball was born in Seattle, Washington, on July 24, 1892. One of four children in a prominent middle-class Black family, Alice's father, James Presley, was a lawyer, photographer, and newspaper editor for the *Colored Citizen*. Her mother, Laura Louise (Howard) Ball, was also a photographer. Her grandfather had been a photographer too: one of the first Black Americans to use daguerreotype, the process of printing photographs onto metal plates. The family's expertise in photography inspired Alice's love for chemistry, as it involved working with mercury vapors and iodine-sensitized silver plates.

Alice and her family moved to Honolulu, Hawai'i, in 1903, then returned to Seattle in 1904, where Alice attended

Alice Augusta Ball, master's degree graduation photograph, University of Hawai'i, 1915.

Seattle High School and achieved top grades in the sciences. After graduating in 1910, Alice enrolled at the University of Washington, where she earned her first bachelor's degree in pharmaceutical chemistry in 1912 and a second in pharmacy science two years later.

In 1914 Alice coauthored a paper with her professor Williams Dehn titled "Benzoylations in Ether Solution"; it was published in the *Journal of the American Chemical Society*. This speaks to Alice's enormous talent, because in the early 1900s, it was rare for a woman, much less a Black woman, to have her work published in such a prestigious scientific journal, rarer still for a professor to give authorship credit to a student.

After college, Ball was offered scholarships to attend graduate school by the University of California, Berkeley and the College of Hawai'i (now the University of Hawai'i). She chose Hawai'i and, in 1915, earned a master's degree in chemistry. She was the first woman and first Black person at the school to earn a master's degree and the first Black person to earn the title of "research chemist and instructor" in the school's chemistry department.

Alice's master's thesis involved identifying the chemical makeup of the kava plant, a crop known to have medicinal benefits. Chemists in the early 1900s often focused their research on identifying active ingredients in medicinal plants so the newly established pharmaceutical industry could develop and sell synthetic versions. Alice's work on the kava plant attracted the attention of Harry T. Hollmann, then acting assistant surgeon at the Leprosy Investigation Station of the US Public Health Service in Hawai'i. Hollmann asked Alice to work with him to identify the chemical composition of chaulmoogra oil, which had been used for hundreds of years as a treatment for leprosy, an illness known today as Hansen's disease. Chaulmoogra oil was difficult to use because it was thick and sticky and could not be injected into the human body. Ingesting the oil was also problematic because the taste was terrible and made patients vomit. Hollmann hoped that by identifying the oil's chemical properties, a more user-friendly synthetic version could be developed.

People who suffered from leprosy in the early 1900s were social pariahs. Many were exiled to the Hawaiian island of Molokai to keep them from coming into contact with the general public. They typically stayed on the island with other leprosy patients until they died.

Alice knew about Molokai and wanted to help the people who were suffering. At age twenty-three she accepted Hollmann's offer and began studying chaulmoogra oil in addition to teaching and doing other research at the University of Hawai'i.

Chaulmoogra tree fruit. pisitpong2017/Shutterstock.

Within a year, Alice had identified the chemical properties of chaulmoogra oil and developed a water-soluble form that could be injected into the human body. She created it by isolating certain compounds and modifying them to eliminate the oil's thick, sticky qualities. Alice was excited, but before she was able to publish a paper on her work, she became ill from exposure to chlorine in her laboratory. In 1916, at only twenty-four years old, she left Hawai'i and returned home to Seattle, where she died a few months later.

After Alice's death, a Harvard-trained chemist named Arthur Dean took over her work. Dean was both dean of the college (he would later become university president) and Alice's graduate adviser. He was familiar with Alice's research and understood why her discovery of injectable chaulmoogra oil was so groundbreaking. By 1919 Dean was producing and selling large quantities of Alice's invention. He even wrote an article detailing how the oil had been modified to make it injectable and said that *his* findings had confirmed the efficacy of the treatment. He never acknowledged Alice as the inventor, nor did Dean credit her work or mention her name in any of the papers he published on injectable chaulmoogra oil, instead calling it the "Dean method."

Hollmann tried to correct Dean's wrongful claims by publishing a paper in 1922 that gave credit to Alice. He referred to the injectable form of chaulmoogra oil as the "Ball method" and explained how Alice had invented the treatment. Dean rebuffed Hollmann's claims, saying his work was a substantial improvement over Alice's method because he used a distillation process to refine the oil, but Hollmann proved otherwise in a section of his paper titled "Ball's Method of Making Ethyl Esters of the Fatty Acids of Chaulmoogra Oil." Hollmann wrote, "I cannot see that there is any improvement whatsoever over the original technique as worked out by Miss Ball. The original method will allow any physician in any asylum for lepers in the world, with a little study, to isolate and use the ethyl esters of chaulmoogra fatty acids in treating his cases, while the complicated distillation *in vacuo* [the method developed by Dean] will require very delicate, and not always obtainable, apparatus."

Plaque honoring Alice under a chaulmoogra tree on the campus of the University of Hawai‘i.

Despite Hollmann's efforts, Alice was largely ignored in the written history of medical treatments for leprosy until the 1970s, when two professors at the University of Hawai‘i found records of Ball's research. They published papers about her work in the hope she would get the recognition she deserved, but nothing changed. Alice's work remained obscure until 2000, when the University of Hawai‘i installed a plaque in her name under a chaulmoogra tree that had been planted in Alice's honor. Hawai‘i's former lieutenant governor Mazie Hirono attended the ceremony and declared February 29 "Alice Ball Day." It was an odd date, as it meant that Alice would be remembered only every four years.

The truth about Dean's fraud became more widely known in 2004, when a scholar at the University of Hawai‘i named Paul Wermager gave a lecture and quoted from a 1921 newspaper interview in which Dean talked about the discovery of injectable chaulmoogra oil. Wermager criticized Dean for crediting Hollmann and a few others, but not Alice.

A few years later, in 2007, the Board of Regents at the University of Hawai'i recognized Alice again by giving her its highest honor, the Medal of Distinction. Then, in 2016, *Hawai'i Magazine* named Alice one of the most influential women in Hawaiian history. In 2018 the city of Seattle, Washington, named a new park after her. Even in Europe, Alice is finally getting the credit she deserves: in 2019 the London School of Tropical Medicine and Hygiene added Alice's name in stone, in huge letters, to the exterior of its building. The honor was once limited to men who had made important contributions to science, but Alice's name now appears alongside Marie Curie's. In February 2020 a short film titled *The Ball Method* premiered at the Pan African Film Festival. Later that year, a satellite was named for Alice.

In 2022 Alice was honored for a third time by the University of Hawai'i, and Governor David Ige presented a proclamation at the ceremony, declaring February 28, rather than February 29, Alice Augusta Ball Day. Alice is now celebrated every year.

Despite all the recent accolades, students at the University of Hawai'i are pressing for more to be done to hold the school's former president accountable for his lies. One idea is to remove Dean's name from a building on campus, currently known as Dean Hall, and rename it Alice Ball Hall. The students find it offensive, as they should, that an entire building is named for a thief, while Alice has but a plaque under a tree.

Learn More

Abele, Dagmawi, dir. *The Ball Method*. Film. 2020. Available on streaming services.

Brewster, Carissa D. "How the Woman Who Found a Leprosy Treatment Was Almost Lost to History." *National Geographic*, February 28, 2018. https://www.nationalgeographic.com/science/article/alice-ball-leprosy-hansens-disease-hawaii-womens-history-science.

20

SHE GREATLY IMPROVED HER HUSBAND'S INVENTION, BUT HE GOT THE PATENT, AND HE WAS DEAD

Most great ideas are built on the work of others, so determining whether someone is entitled to credit isn't usually a black-or-white issue, but in Martha Coston's case, it is. Martha added substantial value to her husband's idea for signal flares, but only he got the patent, even though he was dead.

Martha Jane Coston was born Martha Hunt on December 12, 1826, in Baltimore, Maryland. She moved to Pennsylvania as a child and at age sixteen eloped with a twenty-one-year-old inventor named Benjamin Franklin Coston (no relation to *that* Benjamin Franklin). Benjamin became director of the US Naval Research Lab in Washington, DC, where he invented a small rocket that could send visual signals at night from one ship to another and from ship to shore. He resigned from the navy in 1847 after a disagreement about how much they should pay him for one of his other inventions. Benjamin then became president of the Boston Gas Company, where he worked for only a year before becoming sick from exposure to toxic chemicals. He died in 1848, still in his twenties.

Martha was left to raise four children on her own, though within two years of Benjamin's death, two of her children

Martha Coston, 1886.

died, as did her mother. Struggling emotionally and financially, Martha began reading through her husband's papers and discovered notes he had written about his idea for a nighttime signal flare. In her autobiography, Martha wrote, "I came upon a large envelope containing papers and a skilfully drawn plan of signals to be used at sea, at night for the same purpose of communication that flags are used by day."[1] Benjamin's notes explained that each signal was correlated with a number and a letter and that this code enabled people to spell out information by launching colored flares into the air in a particular order. Martha knew the idea had great potential; she started thinking about how to turn it into an actual product.

Martha's first attempt to construct flares using Benjamin's notes did not work. She had only a limited understanding

1. Martha J. Coston, *A Signal Success: The Work and Travels of Mrs. Martha J. Coston* (1886; repr., Whitefish, MT: Kessinger, 2007), 38.

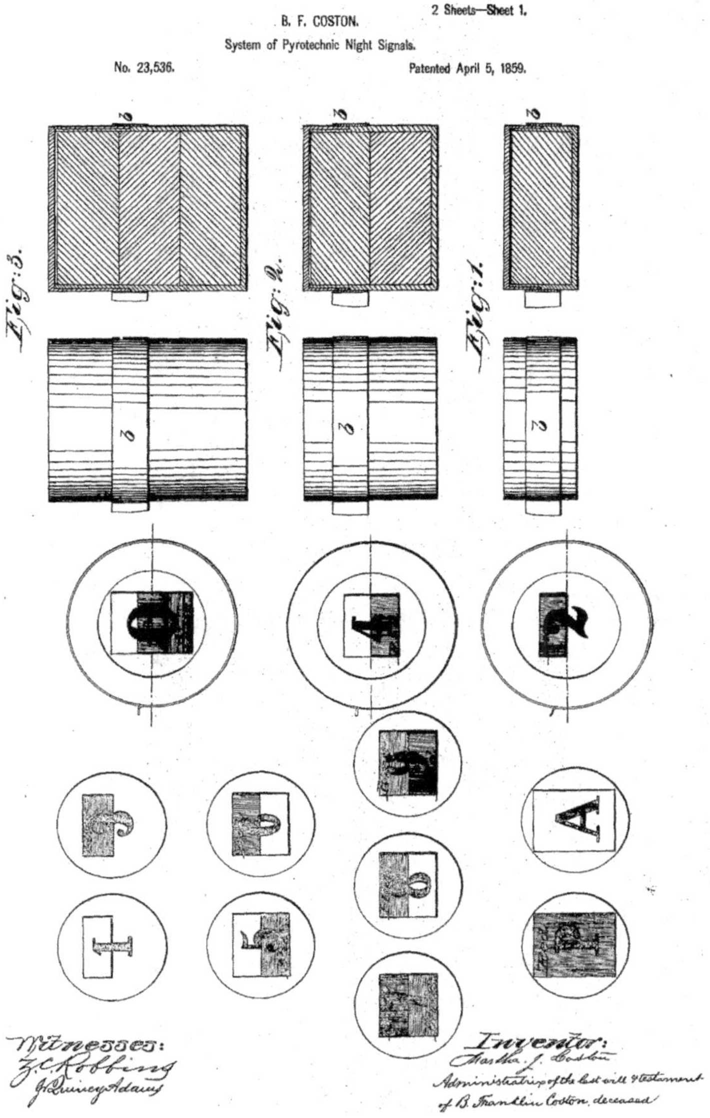

B. F. COSTON. 2 Sheets—Sheet 1.

System of Pyrotechnic Night Signals.

No. 23,536. Patented April 5, 1859.

Fig: 3. Fig: 2. Fig: 1.

Witnesses:
Z. C. Robbins
J. Quincy Adams

Inventor:
Martha J. Coston
Administratrix of the last will & testament of B. Franklin Coston, deceased

Martha's patent drawing for her signal flares. Patent 23536, 1859. Courtesy US Patent Office.

of the technology, so she hired chemists and other experts who explained that she would need several different flare colors for the system to work. Over the next several years, she developed a vivid red flare and a bright white one, but she needed at least one more color for the system to work, and her efforts to create a bright enough blue had been unsuccessful.

Martha finally came up with an idea for how to develop a bright blue flare while watching fireworks in New York in 1858. They had many colors and were both bright and highly tinted, unlike any she had seen before. She sent letters to several pyrotechnic experts in New York asking if they could produce a bright blue flare for her, though she did not tell them why she needed it. She signed her letters using a man's name, fearing they would not respond if they knew she was a woman. Within two weeks, Martha received a package in the mail containing sample flares. She drove to a mountain with a friend and burned them to see how bright they were. They were green rather than blue, but Martha was impressed with the vividness of the color, so she hired the man who sent them to her, then founded the Coston Manufacturing Company and began manufacturing the signal flare system herself.

Martha applied for a patent and described herself as the "INVENTOR" in the signature line, but in the narrative, she also said Benjamin was the "original inventor." Underneath her name, she identified herself as "Administratrix of the last will and testament" of her deceased husband. When the patent was granted on April 5, 1859, it was granted to her only in her capacity as administratrix of Benjamin's estate.

The navy was immediately interested in Martha's flares, describing them as far superior to any other signaling system. In 1859 it offered to buy Martha's patent but never followed through. Martha then traveled to Europe and obtained patents in England, France, Italy, Austria, Denmark, Sweden, and the Netherlands. When she returned to the United States in 1861, she went to Washington, DC, and persuaded Congress to purchase her patent so the military could use her invention during the impending Civil War. Congress agreed and, on August 5, 1861, authorized the navy to purchase the patent for $20,000, half of what Martha originally demanded. The

Admiral Porter's Fleet Celebrating the Surrender of Fort Fisher. Originally published in *Harper's Weekly,* February 4, 1865.

navy then bought the flares from Martha's company, but at a steep discount; it promised to compensate her fully after the war ended.

Martha's signal flare system was used extensively during the Civil War. Confederate ships were captured thanks to the ability of Union soldiers to use the flares to communicate with one another. Union admiral David Porter wrote to Martha about how valuable her invention was: "The signals by night are very much more useful than the signals by day made with flags, for at night the signals can be so plainly read that mistakes are impossible, and a commander-in-chief can keep up a conversation with one of his vessels." Martha's flares were especially helpful for naval operations during the battle of Fort Fisher in North Carolina from January 13 to 15, 1865. Fort Fisher was the last remaining port of the Confederacy. To immobilize it, Admiral Porter organized a nighttime attack by land and sea forces, using Martha's flares to coordinate and communicate tactics and strategy. When Fort Fisher fell, Admiral Porter ordered his soldiers to celebrate by "burning the Coston Signals at all the yard-arms." A drawing of the celebration featuring Martha's flares shooting high above the water at Fort Fisher was published in *Harper's Weekly* on February 4, 1865.

COSTON'S MARINE SIGNALS

Percussion or Friction

The only signal recognized by the British Board of Trade in their report, and is used exclusively by the United States Government.

Distress Outfits for lifeboats in compliance with the rules and regulations of the Board of Steamboat Inspectors; friction or percussion.

Fog, Pilot and Distress Signals, all different steamship and yacht club distinguishing signals, friction or percussion, also regulation ship rockets and staves.

WATER LIGHTS

For Life Buoy, Embarkation or Deck Flares.

Distinguishing colors arranged and registered.

Send for our pamphlet entitled "Communication at Night on the Road at Sea."

Highest award, Gold Medal and Diploma, Jamestown Exposition, 1907.

Originators and largest manufacturers of marine night signals in the world.

COSTON SIGNAL CO., Inc.

7 Water St. **New York**

Entrance on Moore St. Telephone 3454 Broad

Deliveries made by Steam Lighters Day or Night

Advertisement for Martha's signal flares in *Master, Mate & Pilot* magazine, 1913.

In 1871 Martha obtained another patent, this time in her own name, for an improved version of the signal flares that used a twist-ignition system. She sold them not only to the navy but also to yacht clubs, shipping companies, and the US Coast Guard (then known as the US Lifesaving Service).

Martha estimated that the navy owed her $120,000 by the time the Civil War ended. She demanded payment in full but was offered only $15,000.

While Martha was struggling to get paid, the Constitution was being amended, and in 1868 the Fourteenth Amendment was adopted, granting to all "persons" the equal protection of the laws, which of course would include contract laws. Martha might have benefited in her contract dispute with the navy, but the US Supreme Court repeatedly refused to recognize women as persons with equal protection rights. The Supreme Court's dim view of women no doubt contributed to the navy's refusal to pay Martha what she was owed.

Despite her many challenges, Martha's company was successful. The US government continued using her signal flares until the mid-twentieth century, mostly for signaling between ships and summoning help at sea when people needed rescue. Conservative estimates credit Martha's invention with saving thousands of lives.

Martha died in 1904, though her company continued into the 1980s. She was inducted into the National Inventors Hall of Fame in 2006. Her husband, Benjamin, was never inducted.

Learn More

Coston, Martha J. *A Signal Success: The Work and Travels of Mrs. Martha J. Coston.* 1886; reprint, Whitefish, MT: Kessinger, 2007.

"Martha Coston: Inventor of Night Signal Flares for the US Navy." *History of American Women* (blog), n.d. https://www.womenhistoryblog.com/2006/12/martha-coston.html.

21

THE COUPLE WAS EQUALLY RENOWNED, YET ONLY HE GOT THE PRIZE, BECAUSE SHE WROTE A FEMINIST ESSAY

Imagine that you have been working with your spouse in the same profession for a long time. You're both renowned in your field, and both names are in the title of your business. If anything, you're a bit more talented than your spouse. Now imagine that an organization that gives out prestigious awards has informed you that it intends to honor your company. You are elated and proud—until the organization tells you that it can give the prize to only one person, and it will be giving the prize to your spouse.

That's exactly what happened to architect Denise Scott Brown.

Denise Scott Brown was born Denise Lakofski in South Africa on October 3, 1931, to Simon and Phyllis Lakofski. From the time she was five years old, she knew she wanted to be an architect, following in the footsteps of her mother, who had studied architecture.

Denise attended Kingsmead College from 1948 to 1952, then studied at the University of the Witwatersrand in South Africa, where she met and later married Robert Scott Brown. She then traveled to England, where she worked for well-

Denise Scott Brown, photographed in her home, 1978. Photograph copyright Lynn Gilbert. Reproduced under a Creative Commons Attribution-Share Alike 4.0 International license, https://creativecommons.org/licenses/by-sa/4.0/deed.en.

known modernist architect Frederick Gibberd and studied at the prestigious Architectural Association School of Architecture (AASA). The AASA had a reputation for being very supportive of women in architecture.

In 1958 Denise and Robert moved to the United States to attend graduate school at the University of Pennsylvania. A year later, Robert died in a car accident. Denise finished her master's degree in city planning in 1960 and started teaching while completing a second master's degree in architecture.

At a faculty meeting to discuss the proposed demolition of a library, Denise argued in favor of keeping the building because it had been designed by famed architect Frank Furness. One of the other faculty members at the meeting was an architect named Robert Venturi. They began dating and, in 1962, started working and teaching together, until Denise left in 1965 to teach in California.

Denise taught at the University of California, Berkeley until she was hired to cochair the Urban Design Program at the University of California, Los Angeles. She and Robert married in 1967, and Denise returned to Pennsylvania, where Robert had opened his own architecture firm, Venturi and Rauch. She joined the firm as a principal and headed up the planning department.

In 1970 Denise and Robert began teaching at Yale University's School of Architecture and Design. Two years later, they coauthored a book with Steven Izenour titled *Learning from Las Vegas: The Forgotten Symbolism of Architectural Form*. It was a compilation of architectural studies of the Las Vegas strip on which Denise and Robert had worked with their students at Yale.

Denise's architectural style emphasized environmental and cultural concerns. This reflected the fact that she was trained as both an architect and a planner; Robert was only an architect. As a team, they approached projects from a multifaceted perspective, taking into account building design as well as functionality for the space. For example, when planning a campus expansion project for Dartmouth College, they studied not only how to expand the campus by constructing certain buildings but also how to do so with due

The Seattle Art Museum. Courtesy Cliff from Arlington, VA. Reproduced under a Creative Commons Attribution 2.0 Generic license, https://creativecommons.org/licenses/by/2.0/.

regard for the future needs of wilderness around the school. They were known as anti-elitist architects who respected the environment and culture, as well as population trends and patterns.

In 1980 Denise became a named partner in Robert's firm, by which time they were both very successful and well known as visionary architects. They were regularly commissioned to design buildings for academic and civic institutions in the United States and around the world, including the Sainsbury Wing of London's National Gallery and the Seattle Art Museum. In 1985 they won the Architecture Firm Award, the most prestigious prize given by the American Institute of Architects to a firm that produces notable work for at least ten years.

By this time, Denise had published several books with Robert. She had also published many articles and won numerous awards and honorary degrees.

In 1989 Denise published an essay titled "Room at the Top? Sexism and the Star System in Architecture." It described her struggle to be recognized as an equal partner, at her firm and in general in the male-dominated architectural profession. Although she originally wrote the essay in 1975, Denise did not initially publish it because she was worried that it might damage her career. It was critical of architecture's treatment of women and described several instances in which Denise's work was credited to her husband. Midway through, Denise wrote bluntly of the profession's hierarchy, "The architectural prima donnas are all male."

Only two years after the essay was published, Robert and Denise learned that their firm would be honored with the Pritzker Prize. The Pritzker recognizes architects whose work "demonstrates a combination of talent, vision, and commitment, which has produced consistent and significant contributions to humanity and the built environment through the art of architecture." It comes with a $100,000 cash award and is often called "Architecture's Nobel." It was an important award, but the Prize Committee said that only Robert would be recognized. Offended by the snub, Denise refused to attend the ceremony. Robert asked that the award be given to both of them, but his request was denied, and he accepted the honor in Denise's absence.

The prestigious Pritzker Prize in Architecture that was given to Denise's husband. The Hyatt Foundation/Pritzker Architecture Prize. Used with permission.

Some said the sponsor of the Pritzker Prize, the Hyatt Foundation, declined to honor Denise because it was offended by her essay about sexism in architecture. The Foundation claimed publicly that it could honor only one architect at a time, but the prize had been given to two men three years earlier and was again given to two men a few years later, in 2001.

The scandal went largely unnoticed until 2013, when a student organization at the Harvard Graduate School of Design, known as Women in Design, started a petition demanding that Denise be recognized for her equal right to claim the 1991 Pritzker Prize alongside her husband. The petition drew twenty thousand signatures from around the world, but the Hyatt Foundation did not budge. In 2017 Denise won the Jane Drew Prize, which is given annually to a person who shows innovation, diversity, and inclusiveness in architecture. The Jane Drew Prize is now part of the W Awards, a program of the *Architectural Review* and *Architects' Journal* that recognizes a person's "contribution to the status of women in architecture." During her acceptance speech, Denise talked about the Pritzker Prize controversy and said the fact that twenty thousand people supported a petition on her behalf was reward enough.

The disrespect Denise suffered inspired her to become an advocate for women in architecture. She has spoken out extensively about sex discrimination in the profession and remains a dedicated voice for women in architecture today.

Learn More

Tamas, Andrea. "Interview: Robert Venturi and Denise Scott Brown." *Arch Daily,* April 25, 2011. https://www.archdaily.com/130389/interview-robert-venturi-denise-scott-brown-by-andrea-tamas.

22

EVEN AS A STUDENT, SHE DESERVED MORE CREDIT

Even if you've never been a graduate student, you know something about what they do. In addition to teaching and studying, they often spend long hours in laboratories, doing tedious tasks for little or no pay on behalf of a lab director who hopes to publish an academic paper one day. Students' names might be listed as secondary authors of the lab director's paper, but they don't expect a lot of accolades for doing the work someone else tells them to do.

The rules get murky, however, when a student discovers something on her own. Such is the story of astrophysicist Jocelyn Bell-Burnell, who discovered pulsar stars in 1967 while working for a lab director who wasn't even looking for pulsars. It was such an important scientific achievement that it earned a Nobel Prize in 1974, but the honor went to two men instead of to Bell-Burnell.

Jocelyn Bell was born on July 15, 1943, to G. Philip and M. Allison Bell. Raised in the countryside of Northern Ireland with a younger brother and two younger sisters, Jocelyn often visited the Armagh Planetarium, which her father had designed and helped to build. The people she met at the planetarium inspired her to become an astronomer.

Jocelyn Bell-Burnell, 1967, when she discovered the first pulsar. Courtesy Roger W. Haworth.

Jocelyn attended prep school at Lurgan College from 1948 to 1956, at a time when girls were expected to study cooking and cross-stitching. She wasn't interested in either, but she was forbidden to study the sciences until her parents challenged the school's sexist policies.

After prep school, Jocelyn failed her college entry exams, so her parents sent her to a Quaker boarding school for girls in England. There she learned physics from an inspirational teacher who encouraged her and made physics seem easy. She graduated in 1961 and enrolled at the University of Glasgow, from which she graduated with honors in 1965 with a bachelor's degree in natural philosophy (philosophical study of physics). Jocelyn was then accepted into a PhD program at a women-only college known as New Hall (now Murray Edwards College) at the University of Cambridge. She was assigned to the radio astronomy group, where her adviser was Antony Hewish. Together with Hewish, Jocelyn constructed a special telescope that could observe and map radioactive signals in the sky. Once it was built, Jocelyn was responsible for monitoring and analyzing the telescope's printed data to look for quasars, which are extremely bright objects that form the center of galaxies.

While reviewing data on August 6, 1967, Jocelyn detected a strange radio signal that she knew was not a quasar. She described it to Hewish as a "bit of scruff," but he dismissed it as a meaningless anomaly caused by man-made interference. Jocelyn was not so sure. She carefully analyzed hundreds of pages of complicated data every day for months and, on November 28, determined that the "scruff" was pulsing at a rate of about one pulse every one and one-third seconds. Her persistence paid off—Jocelyn discovered a never-before-seen star, now known as a pulsar.

Pulsars are highly magnetized stars that rotate in a regular pattern. During their rotation, they emit electromagnetic radiation, which can be observed only while the stars are facing Earth. This gives the stars their pulsing appearance.

In 1968 Hewish wrote a paper describing the discovery of pulsars. He listed his name as lead author, followed by Jocelyn as second author.

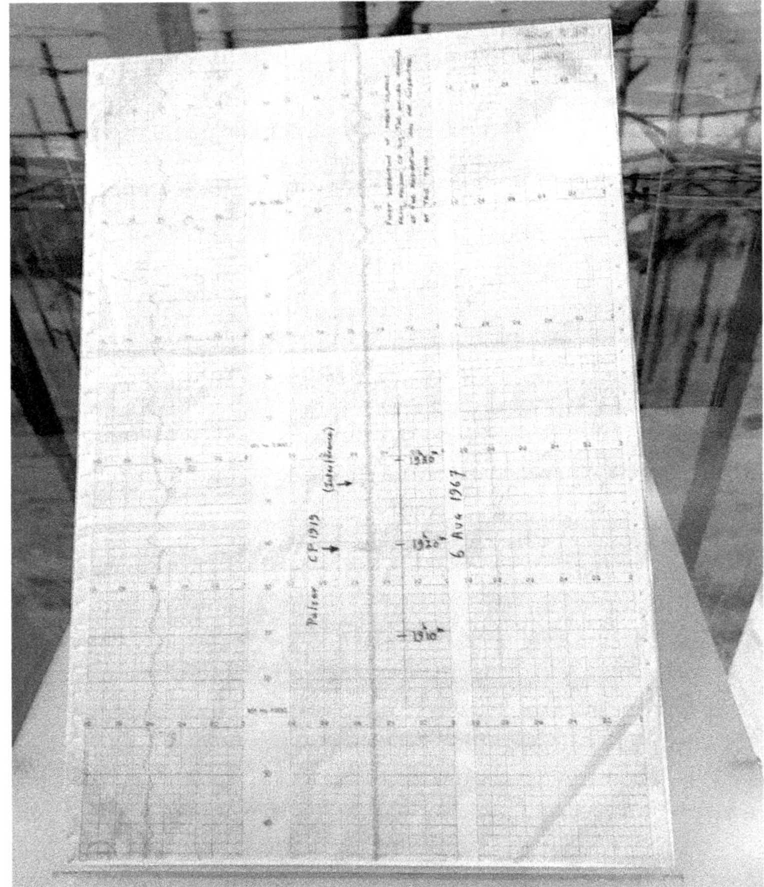

The printed data that Jocelyn analyzed to discover the first pulsar in 1967, exhibited at Cambridge University Library. Courtesy Billthom. Reproduced under a Creative Commons Attribution-Share Alike 4.0 International license, https://creativecommons.org/licenses/by-sa/4.0/deed.en.

While this exciting work was going on, Jocelyn became engaged to Martin Burnell and showed up on campus one day wearing an engagement ring. Some of her colleagues remarked that it would be shameful if she continued working, as it would indicate that her fiancé was unable to provide for the family. Jocelyn changed her last name to Bell-Burnell and started working part-time after the couple married and had a child.

Several years later, Jocelyn's discovery of pulsars won a Nobel Prize, but it went to Hewish and a man named Martin Ryle, rather than to Jocelyn. Ryle was a researcher at the University of Cambridge in the same field as Hewish, but he had no direct involvement in the discovery of pulsars. Nonetheless, the Nobel Committee said the award would go to Hewish and Ryle because Hewish had discovered pulsars and Ryle had developed a technique that allowed multiple sources of data from radio signaling to be combined to produce a single image of an object, such as a star or black hole.

Jocelyn was not offended by the snub, even though she spent two years helping to build the telescope that enabled her to see pulsars, and she alone reviewed and analyzed the data that revealed their existence. Once Hewish realized the importance of Jocelyn's discovery, he excluded her from meetings where he and Ryle strategized about how to handle it.

Jocelyn was modest about her role, saying in 1977, "I believe it would demean Nobel Prizes if they were awarded to research students, except in very exceptional cases, and I do not believe this is one of them." However, years later, she said, "The fact that I was a graduate student and a woman, together, demoted my standing in terms of receiving a Nobel Prize."

Despite being snubbed, Jocelyn enjoyed a long career as an astrophysicist. She worked at the University of Southampton from 1968 to 1973 and at University College London from 1974 to 1982. She then moved to the Royal Observatory in Edinburgh in 1982, where she stayed until 1991. For many years, she also worked as a tutor, consultant, examiner, lecturer, and physics professor for Open University. From 1986 to 1991 Jocelyn was a project manager for the James Clerk Maxwell Telescope at Mauna Kea Observatory, Hawai'i. She also taught as a visiting professor at Princeton University and was appointed dean of science at the University of Bath from 2001 to 2004. She served as president of the Royal Astronomical Society from 2002 to 2004 and as president of the Institute of Physics from 2008 to 2010.

Artist's rendition of a pulsar. More than three thousand pulsars have been identified since Jocelyn discovered the first one in 1967. Courtesy NASA.

In 2018 Jocelyn was awarded the Special Breakthrough Prize in Fundamental Physics. She donated all her prize money, $3 million, "to fund women, under-represented ethnic minority and refugee students to become physics researchers." In that same year, she was appointed chancellor of the University of Dundee.

In 2021 Jocelyn became only the second female recipient of the Copley Medal, which recognizes "outstanding achievements in research in any branch of science." The medal is the oldest surviving scientific award in the world. In July 2022 a new science-themed bank note was issued by Ulster Bank, featuring Jocelyn and other women scientists.

At eighty years old, Jocelyn is still thriving in her field, working as a professor of astrophysics at the University of Oxford and as a Fellow of Mansfield College.

Learn More

James, C. Renée. "Pulsars at 50 Still Going Strong." *Astronomy,* August 16, 2019. https://www.astronomy.com/science/pulsars-at-50-still-going-strong/.

23

IF SHE HADN'T BEEN MARRIED TO THE MAN WHO WON THE NOBEL PRIZE, SHE MIGHT HAVE WON IT HERSELF

Most married women have stories about how things are unfair when it comes to home life, who does the laundry, and so forth. Who hasn't heard a man be praised for cooking or taking care of the children, while women who do the same things get no applause because that's their job?

It's no different for women professionals who work with their husbands. Too often, the man is presumed to be the leader or the more qualified of the pair, especially if the couple works in a male-dominated field. Nobody suffered more from this form of wife discrimination than Esther Lederberg.

Esther Miriam Zimmer was born the oldest of two children in the Bronx, New York, on December 18, 1922, to Orthodox Jewish parents David and Pauline Geller Zimmer. Her father worked in a printing factory and sometimes took Esther with him and taught her how printing machines work. During the Great Depression, Esther's family struggled financially. For lunch they often ate only bread soaked in tomato juice.

Esther went to Evander Childs High School in the Bronx and graduated early in 1938, at age fifteen. She won a

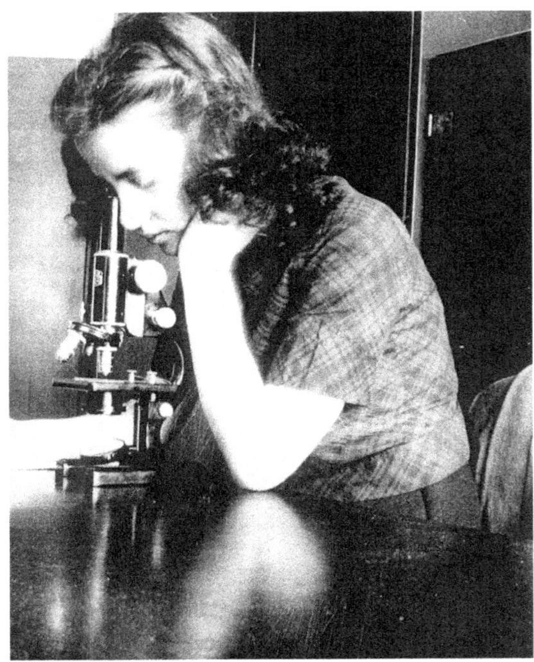

Esther, aged about eighteen years. Copyright the Esther M. Zimmer Lederberg Trust, http://www.estherlederberg.com/.

scholarship to Hunter College, where she initially studied French and literature but switched to biochemistry, despite teachers' warnings that as a woman, she would have difficulty pursuing a career in science.

As a college student, Esther did research at the New York Botanical Gardens under the guidance of well-known plant expert Bernard Ogilvie Dodge. She graduated cum laude in 1942 at age nineteen with a bachelor's degree in genetics.

After graduation, Esther worked for Alexander Hollaender at the Carnegie Institution of Washington's Department of Genetics (now the Cold Spring Harbor Laboratory). Hollaender was among the world's leading experts in radiation biology and genetic mutations. In 1945 Esther and Hollaender coauthored a paper on radiation, X-rays, and genetic mutations.

In 1944 Esther won a fellowship to Stanford University, where she worked with George Wells Beadle and Edward Tatum, a team of scientists that would later win a Nobel Prize in Physiology or Medicine for their work in genetics. When Esther first met Tatum, she asked him to teach her about genetics. He was reluctant but invited her to visit him at his lab the following day. When she arrived, she saw a milk bottle filled with fruit flies; all but one had the same eye color. Esther assumed Tatum wanted her to explain why one fly had a different eye color, so she told him what she thought. Her explanation was so good that Tatum made her his teaching assistant for his genetics class.

Esther later studied at Stanford's Hopkins Marine Station and entered a master's degree program in genetics. Her thesis was titled "Mutant Strains of Neurospora Deficient in Para-Aminobenzoic Acid." She graduated in 1946 and married Joshua Lederberg the same year. She was twenty-three; he was twenty-one. By this time, Tatum was teaching at Yale University, and Joshua was his PhD student. Esther left Stanford and

Esther Lederberg, circa 1977, in her laboratory at Stanford University. Copyright the Esther M. Zimmer Lederberg Trust, http://www.estherlederberg.com/.

worked at Yale's Osborn Botanical Laboratory until Joshua graduated. She then moved with him to the University of Wisconsin, where Joshua became a professor.

Esther began studying for her PhD at the University of Wisconsin in 1946 after being awarded a predoctoral fellowship from the National Cancer Institute. Her thesis was titled "Genetic Control of Mutability in the Bacterium *Escherichia coli*"; her supervisor was well-known geneticist R. A. Brink. She received her PhD in 1950.

Esther continued doing research at the University of Wisconsin throughout the 1950s and was the first scientist to isolate an unusual bacteriophage known as lambda phage. A bacteriophage is a virus that can infect bacteria; lambda phage is a unique type of bacteriophage that acts differently than other bacteriophages.

Esther first observed lambda phage in 1946 as a PhD student. Before then, scientists thought viruses replicated by penetrating cells and reproducing inside them until the cells burst, which would then expose surrounding cells to the virus and infect them until they burst, and so on. Esther's discovery of lambda phage proved that not all bacteriophages were the same because when lambda phage infected *E. coli* bacteria, it reproduced and spread not by bursting a cell but by integrating itself into a cell's genome and creating a mutated organism that could then replicate through ordinary cell division.

In 1953 Esther published a paper explaining her landmark work on lambda phage and genetic mutations in the journal *Genetics*. She described how she first observed lambda phage in 1946, the same year Joshua published his first paper on genetic mutations. Joshua had discouraged Esther from doing follow-up research on lambda phage in 1946 because, he said, it would distract her from completing her dissertation and her adviser, Brink, would not understand its significance.

Esther's work in the 1950s was prolific; she published many papers on virus replication and codiscovered the *E. coli* F factor (fertility factor) with famed geneticist Luigi Luca Cavalli-Sforza. The F factor is what allows genes to be transferred from a bacterium that has the F factor to another bacterium that does not. She also codiscovered with Joshua the way genetic material recombines to produce new genetic material, and she identified the genetic mechanisms of specialized transduction, which is the process by which certain genes are transferred from one bacterium to another by a virus.

Esther even developed a new technique for studying the behavior of bacteria, known as replica plating. Though newer techniques have since been developed, replica plating allowed researchers to copy bacterial colonies from a master plate and place them onto different plates or petri dishes. It was like making a photocopy not only of bacteria but also of their precise locations on the master plate. Joshua worked with Esther on replica plating, but it was Esther who came up with the idea, inspired by her experiences as a child learning about the printing process at her father's factory.

The ability to copy a master plate allowed researchers to learn important information about how bacteria function in response to different stimuli. For example, scientists could add a particular antibiotic to a petri dish to see whether certain bacteria from the master plate died off or became resistant. They could then add other antibiotics to the same colony in a different petri dish and compare the results. This enabled scientists to determine which combination of antibiotics successfully eradicated a certain bacterial colony. Geneticists around the world used replica plating during the latter part of the twentieth century.

Replica plating helped Esther and Joshua demonstrate that antibiotic-resistant mutant organisms could evolve even in the absence of antibiotics. In other words, mutations were not caused solely by the killing off of certain bacteria by antibiotics. Spontaneous mutations had been described previously by other scientists using mathematical equations. The Lederbergs were the first to show visibly how it happens.

In 1956 Esther and Joshua were jointly awarded the Pasteur Medal by the Society of Illinois Bacteriologists for their foundational work on bacterial genetics. Thereafter, Esther gave talks at many prestigious international conferences, including the 1957 Symposium of Bacterial and Viral Genetics in Canberra, Australia, and the tenth International Congress of Genetics in Montreal, Canada, in 1958. Later that same year, Joshua

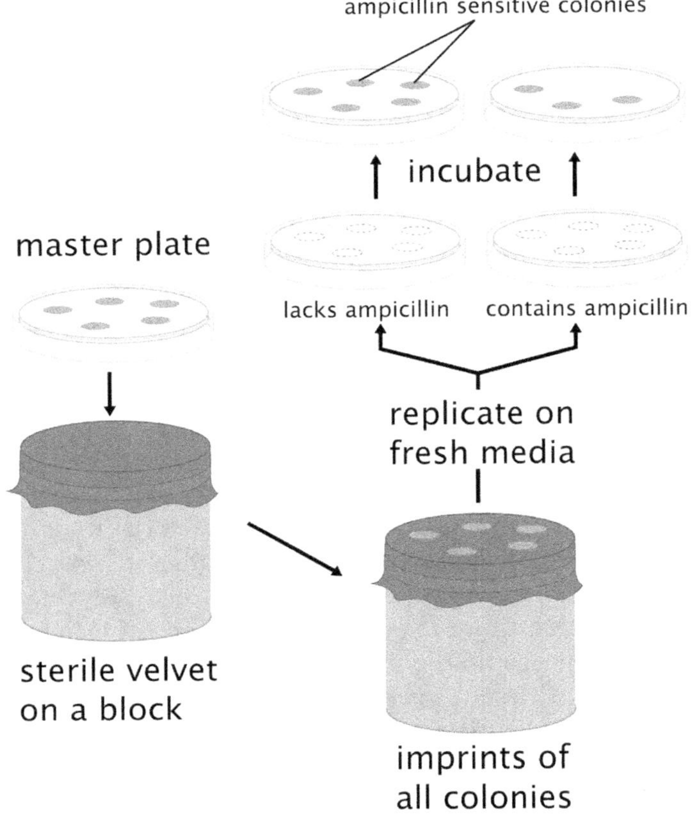

Artist's rendition of replica plating. Courtesy Histidine. Reproduced under a Creative Commons Attribution-ShareAlike 3.0 Unported license, https://creativecommons.org/licenses/by-sa/3.0.

learned that he alone would be awarded the Nobel Prize for discoveries related to how bacteria mutate and exchange genetic material. Esther was ignored, though she had done seminal work in the same field. At the award ceremony in Sweden, Esther was treated like the wife of a Nobel Prize winner rather than as a world-renowned scientist in her own right. Research centers then began recruiting Joshua, but not Esther, to work with them.

Esther and Joshua returned to Stanford in 1959, where Esther remained a research scientist for the rest of her life. She headed up the Plasmid Reference Center at the Stanford School of Medicine from 1976 to 1986, then retired but continued to work as a volunteer.

Esther has widely been described as "a genius in the lab" and a pioneer research scientist, but she faced significant challenges as a woman not only from the scientific community but also from her own husband. For example, after discouraging Esther from doing follow-up work on her observations of lambda phage in 1946, Joshua did follow-up work himself and published papers on the topic, which led to his Nobel Prize in 1958. The Nobel Prize website states that Joshua won because of his work on DNA mutations and recombinations, which is what Esther had discovered with lambda phage in 1946 and with the F factor in *E. coli* in 1947, when she showed that organisms can mix their genetic material, mutate, and produce entirely new organisms. One of Esther's papers, "The Mutability of Several Lacmutants of *Escherichia coli*," was published in 1948, the same year Joshua published a paper on a similar topic. Yet most textbooks on the subject highlight only Joshua's work.

Despite the enormous importance of her work, Esther was never offered a tenure-track position at any university, nor was she invited to submit a chapter for the 1966 book *Phage and the Origins of Molecular Biology*, which was a commemorative book on the topic of molecular biology. According to science historian Pnina Abir-Am, Esther's exclusion was "incomprehensible" because her discoveries in the field of bacteriophage genetics were so important.[1] Abir-Am and many others attribute Esther's exclusion to sexism in science, exacerbated by the fact that she was married to a man who was renowned in the same field. Esther was a highly accomplished scientist who published fifteen scientific papers as

1. Pnina G. Abir-Am, "The First American and French Commemorations in Molecular Biology: From Collective Memory to Comparative History," *Osiris* 14 (1999): 324–70, https://doi.org/10.1086/649312.

sole author and another twenty-three as a coauthor with others, yet she was often treated as her husband's assistant.

Joshua did sometimes acknowledge Esther's work. For example, at the 1951 Cold Spring Harbor Symposium where he presented his paper on recombinant DNA, he told the audience that Esther was the second author on his paper, and he talked about her work on genetic mutations and *E. coli.* When Joshua won the Eli Lilly Prize in 1953, he told a reporter that "Esther should have been in on that too." However, during his Nobel Prize acceptance speech only a few years later in 1958, he said he had "enjoyed the companionship of many colleagues, above all my wife," as if Esther's role in his work was nothing more than official hand-holder. And he did not acknowledge her at all when he wrote about his work on recombinant DNA.

Esther and Joshua's marriage fell apart after the Nobel Prize disaster. Esther struggled in relative obscurity as a research scientist at Stanford, never even earning a Nobel Prize nomination, while her husband in 1959 was appointed head of the genetics department at Stanford. Several years later, Esther and two other women complained to the dean of Stanford School of Medicine about the lack of women professors but were told that no woman had published enough scholarly papers to qualify for a professorship there. When Esther pointed out than many of the male professors had published even fewer papers, she was told that there wasn't any money to hire a woman. Esther reminded the dean of public funding that had been earmarked for hiring women professors, but the dean said that money would be used to promote minorities who were protesting and creating problems for Stanford. Esther eventually agreed to accept an untenured position, while the other women insisted on tenure-track positions or nothing. Esther was the only one who got a professorship—it was in the Department of Microbiology and Immunology, but it was untenured.

Esther divorced Joshua in 1968, after which she struggled even more at Stanford. Joshua openly snubbed her on campus, and in 1974 she was demoted to adjunct professor.

In 1989 Esther met a man named Matthew Simon. They married in 1993 and remained married for the rest of Esther's life.

When Esther died in California in 2006 at age eighty-three, Joshua offered no condolences and paid Esther no tributes, though his colleagues at Stanford did. Noted Stanford biologist Stanley Falkow said that Esther's "independent seminal contributions in Joshua's laboratory . . . surely led, in part, to his Nobel Prize." Esther's husband, Matthew Simon, feels the same way and has dedicated himself to developing the Esther M. Zimmer Lederberg Memorial Website, to honor Esther's work and ensure that she gets the credit she deserves. Simon has spent more than fifteen years organizing and posting information online to make it easier for people to appreciate the significance of Esther's work and understand the disrespect she suffered not only because she was a woman but also because she was married to a man who took advantage of her brilliance while undermining her significance. Maybe the Nobel Committee will understand this one day and make things right.

Learn More

Esther M. Zimmer Lederberg Memorial Website, http://www.estherlederberg.com/.

Schindler, Thomas E. *A Hidden Legacy: The Life and Work of Esther Zimmer Lederberg*. Oxford: Oxford University Press, 2021.

24

SHE GAVE HER INVENTION AWAY TO HELP OTHERS, THEN TWO MEN PATENTED IT

Have you ever given something away out of the goodness of your heart, only to have someone downplay your generosity or question your motive? Even worse, has anyone ever grabbed the spotlight when you deserved it because he knew you were not the type to speak up for yourself? This is exactly what happened when Tabitha Babbitt invented the circular saw. She gave her design away rather than getting a patent for it because she was part of a Shaker religious community in which personal pride was discouraged. Two men who saw Tabitha's design in a Shaker newsletter knew it wasn't patented, so they stole it and patented it themselves.

Sarah Babbitt was born on December 9, 1779, in Hardwick, Massachusetts, to Seth and Elizabeth Babbitt. Known as Tabitha, Sarah became a member of the Shaker religious community in 1793, at age thirteen. The Shakers were founded in England around 1747 as a breakaway group from the Quakers.

Shakers are known for their communal lifestyle, pacifism, simple living, and commitment to equality of the races and sexes. They believe God is both male and female, and they

Portrait of a woman believed to be Sarah "Tabitha" Babbitt, artist unknown.

recognize no boundaries between people based on race, sex, social class, or education. Women serve in positions of leadership, and authority is shared by male elders and female eldresses. Frugal and humble, members are urged to give up all worldly goods.

When the Shakers first came to America in 1774, they settled in New York before branching out. Between 1787 and 1792, Shakers established chapters in Massachusetts, Connecticut,

New Hampshire, and Maine, eventually expanding west to Kentucky, Ohio, and Indiana. Over time, they established more than twenty communities across the United States.

Although the Shakers considered men and women to be equals, they divided labor along gendered lines, with men working the farms while women did spinning, weaving, and baking. They made and sold furniture, baskets, and fabrics. They also grew and sold medicinal herbs and food.

In 1810 Tabitha was working as a weaver in a Shaker community in the small town of Harvard, Massachusetts, alongside Shaker men who worked in a sawmill. She noticed the men using a two-person whipsaw to cut logs by pulling it back and forth. Tabitha thought that this was inefficient and that a circular saw would be better because it would continuously cut wood, thus accomplishing more with less manpower. It was a smart idea, but she had to find a way to make it spin. She attached the blade to her spinning wheel and used the power of her foot pedal to keep it turning. She then figured out that the spinning wheel could be attached to waterpower so that no human pedaling was needed. Her design enabled fewer men to cut more lumber with less energy and in a shorter period of time.

After perfecting her invention, Tabitha shared it with the Shaker community. She did not patent it because she wanted it to be widely available for all to use. She believed in the Shaker values of communal living and modesty and did not want to benefit personally.

Tabitha's circular saw design was distributed through Shaker newsletters, and Shaker men began using it in their sawmills. Two men who were not Shakers, August Brunet and J. B. Cochot, saw Tabitha's invention, obtained a patent for it in 1816 (three years after it appeared in a Shaker newsletter), and sold it for profit.

Because Tabitha did not apply for a patent, it is difficult to prove with certainty that she was the original inventor, but her story is credible. Records show that no US patents had been issued for such a circular saw before Tabitha's design was published in Shaker newsletters. (A British man named Samuel Miller had invented a saw with a circular

Tabitha's circular saw.

blade in 1777, but it was patented in England, and it was small. Tabitha's design was larger and more sophisticated.) The *Boston Sunday Globe* published a story about Tabitha inventing the circular saw on October 30, 1898, when it interviewed another member of the Shaker community named Eliza Babbitt. Nothing in the public record indicates that anyone contacted the *Globe* to challenge the story's claim that Tabitha invented the circular saw. Criticisms of Tabitha did not emerge until more than a century later and rest on allegations that no documents exist to prove that she invented the circular saw, but critics fail to offer any explanation for why Tabitha or Eliza Babbitt would lie. Shakers were known as inventors and were well respected as modest, hardworking people with deeply held religious beliefs who frowned on dishonesty. Furthermore, Tabitha is credited with inventing many other things for which she also declined to obtain patents, such as an improved spinning wheel head for a weaver's loom and a process for making false teeth. She also invented a device to create "cut nails," which are nails cut from sheets of steel that have a narrow, angled shape so they can grip wood without splitting it, which was a common problem with cylindrical nails at the time.

Tabitha died in Harvard, Massachusetts, on December 10, 1853, at age seventy-four. She has not been inducted into the

National Inventors Hall of Fame because she declined to patent her inventions.

In 2015 an inventor named Sam Asano cited Tabitha Babbitt and Benjamin Franklin in support of his argument that the Hall of Fame should change its inclusion criteria to recognize inventors who did not obtain patents. At a minimum, the Hall of Fame should give special consideration to inventors, like Tabitha, who felt compelled not to obtain patents because of their religious beliefs. It should also take into account that women back then did not have equal rights under the law, a problem we should *still* take into account today, because women *still* don't have equal rights.

Learn More

Becksvoort, Christian. *The Shaker Legacy: Perspectives on an Enduring Furniture Style.* Newtown, CT: Taunton Press, 1998.

Harrison, Barbara. "The Background of Shaker Furniture." *New York History* 29, no. 3 (1948): 318–26. https://www.jstor.org/stable/43460291.

Author's Note

In my mind's eye, I see these amazing women sitting together somewhere in the universe, sharing stories and smiling, confident that their lives were enriched by curiosity and creativity regardless of the men who took credit for their work. I hope they're glad their stories are being told, though this book gives them short shrift compared to what they deserve. I could have written an entire book on each one of them, but I wanted to tell as many stories as possible and show the commonalities of the women's experiences.

I am not the first to tell these stories, but I am the first to compile them. I found them in a variety of places, and though many took place a long time ago, when women had fewer rights, the problem is ongoing today. Just ask Blair Glaser, who, in 2021, published a piece in the *Huffington Post* describing how a man she met for coffee to talk about her leadership ideas later wrote a book using those very ideas—without attribution. When she confronted him, he claimed not to remember, so she showed him her written work and pointed out that it preceded his book by several years. She also showed him proof that they had discussed her ideas and that his book used her exact phrasing. He was forced to acknowledge his theft and offered to give her credit in the paperback version, but he never did. Blair ended her piece by inviting men to "be more aware, to reflect on their tone and motives when responding to women's contributions, and to make a conscious effort to champion—not steal—women's thoughts." Realizing that nothing would be done to hold the man accountable, Blair concluded, "To focus too much energy on controlling men's behavior is a path of endless frustration."

Blair didn't say why she feels so hopeless about men. Does she think women are naturally vulnerable, or that men are less ethical? After her piece came out, Blair was deluged with stories from other women who had similar tales to tell. I hope this book, like Blair's piece, inspires women to tell more stories, and to look a little harder for stories still untold, but how do we do that? A recent study might help. Researchers at the University of Washington looked at scholarly articles on the topic of neuroscience published between 2005 and 2017 and identified the sex of the authors to see whether men or women were more likely to be listed as first author.[1] The results were, in their words, "dispiriting." They expected about 40 percent of first-named authors to be women because that was the percentage of female postdocs in neuroscience, but only 25 percent were. They explained the disparity by describing several ways in which gender bias is a factor and called on scientific journals to collect data about gender and make them publicly available so the journals can be held accountable. Depressing as it is, the study gives us an opportunity to find untold stories by reaching out to the women who deserved to be listed first and asking them about their experiences. We have to be creative when looking for invisible stories because women have little influence over the institutions that control and produce information, such as higher education, science, religion, media, and law.

Men taking credit for women's work is small potatoes compared to other ways that women suffer, such as rape and domestic abuse, but all stories of injustice help us better understand why women's status as second-class citizens is the

1. "Women Feature Only Rarely as First or Last Authors in Leading Journals," *Nature*, March 28, 2018, https://www.nature.com/articles/d41586-018-03804-2.

primary problem. Women have always been excellent artists, inventors, scientists, and leaders, but until we have full legal equality, we cannot be ensured equal treatment anywhere.

As the world's most influential democracy, the United States should lead by example, but neither of the two major political parties has seriously supported the Equal Rights Amendment (ERA), which would establish women's equality once and for all. First filed with Congress in 1923, the ERA states, "Equality of rights shall not be denied or abridged by the United States or by any State on account of sex." When it was ratified by the last necessary state in January 2020, the Trump administration blocked it and fought against it in a Massachusetts federal court lawsuit and another, similar lawsuit in DC federal court. The Democrats said they supported the ERA, so lots of women voted for Joe Biden in 2020, but after he was elected, his administration also fought against the ERA in court and blocked it the same way the Trump administration had.

Seeing both parties oppose the ERA is painful, but at least women now know that they need to be nonpartisan to achieve full equality. Legendary and brilliant women's rights activist Alice Paul understood this better than anyone. Alice had multiple degrees in law, sociology, and economics. She earned a PhD from the University of Pennsylvania in 1912 with a dissertation titled "The Legal Position of Women in Pennsylvania." She later earned a law degree as well as a master's degree and a doctorate in law.

Alice knew that neither party supported voting rights or equality for women, so she founded the National Woman's Party in 1916 and announced that it would oppose any Democrat or Republican who refused to support women's suffrage and equality regardless of their position on other issues. Her strategy was genius. Women had been fighting for the vote since the 1800s but, in 1916, were not close to succeeding because neither party supported women's suffrage. Women obediently followed one party or the other, so they got stuck in political limbo until Alice came along. By giving women their own party, and making sure it was fiercely nonpartisan, she gave them the leverage they needed to pressure both parties to do the right thing. The Nineteenth Amendment became law only four years after the Woman's Party was formalized. Before Alice's leadership, women's fight for suffrage had limped along for more than seventy years.

Once women had the right to vote, the Woman's Party turned its attention to the fight for equality. Alice wrote the ERA and got it filed with Congress in 1923, but nothing was done because, again, both parties refused to support it. Alice and the Woman's Party remained indefatigable for decades in their fight for the ERA, but most women's groups refused to help. The Woman's Party was still leading the charge during the 1960s civil rights era, when Congress finally began talking about passing the ERA. Public support was strong, but things slowed down when the National Organization for Women (NOW) was founded in 1966 because it announced at its first annual convention that it did not support the ERA. Women were angry and confused. Why would a women's organization be opposed to women's equality?

NOW was pressured to support the ERA, and by the time it was finally scheduled for a congressional hearing in 1971, NOW did testify favorably, though after the ERA passed Congress, NOW did little to help with state ratifications until it was too late. Other seemingly pro-women groups, such as the League of Women Voters, the Feminist Majority, the American Civil Liberties Union, and the National Women's Law Center, similarly either opposed the ERA or did little or nothing to help. It's important to keep these things in mind when deciding which women's groups to support. Groups that do not prioritize the ERA should be viewed skeptically. Smaller, unfunded, lesser-known groups are usually the least partisan and the least corrupt.

Few women's groups today acknowledge how much power the Woman's Party wielded, and only a handful know the story of how the party was destroyed. Over the course of several years in the 1970s and 1980s, the Woman's Party was infiltrated by a small group of hostile members who joined in bad faith. They eventually filed a lawsuit against the party, at the conclusion of which the Woman's Party was dissolved. It exists today only as a nonpolitical, charitable organization that oversees the party's headquarters in Washington, DC—not as a place of political activism but as a national monument and museum. Think about that: the Woman's Party was intentionally dissolved and its headquarters was turned into a museum at exactly the point in time when the fight for equality was gaining steam. The dissolution became final in 2021, but nobody even noticed.

The question now is, will women learn from Alice Paul and unite again in a new iteration of the Woman's Party? Will they find an incorruptible leader like Alice, who understands the importance of nonpartisan activism and single-minded focus on equality? If such an organization is successful and women do one day achieve full equality, will it stop men from harming women and taking credit for their work?

Probably not, but it's a good place to start.

# Acknowledgments

Many people helped me on this journey, mostly by reading a chapter and offering feedback. My father, Ed Murphy, sister Barbara Murphy, daughter Reed, and son Grant listened more than most. Lots of others cheered me on, including my mom, Sandra Cetrone, and many friends. Jim Braude gave sage advice while insisting he wasn't a writer, and Monique Howell at the Indiana Public Library spent time finding usable photographs of Ada Harris after I struck out. Anna Hedgeman's grandson Peter Fayard and Candace Pert's husband, Michael Ruff, gave me permission to use photographs and let me know that Anna and Candace would be delighted with this book because both women cared deeply about women's issues. Ruth Sime reviewed my chapter on Lise Meitner and helped me better understand physics. Coline Jenkins, the great-great-granddaughter of legendary women's rights activist Elizabeth Cady Stanton, shared stories about her family and told me that Elizabeth would have loved this book because she was passionate about women's equality. Denise Scott Brown took the time to read her chapter and talk to me about her amazing life. It's a phone call I will never forget. Holly Monteith edited my work without being heavy-handed and taught me a lot about the publishing business. Most of all, I am grateful to the women in these chapters. In many cases, nothing was done to remedy the injustices they endured; this book at least shines a light on their stories. As I've told many clients over the years who were victimized by abuse, the most important thing they can do is tell.

Questions for Discussion

1. What commonalities do you see among these women? How might they relate to what the women experienced?

2. In many cases, these women were raised by single parents. What effect might it have had on the women who were raised by a man versus by a woman?

3. What sociological factors might have played a role in the willingness of these women to compete in spheres that were unfriendly to women?

4. What factors might have influenced these women to stay silent?

5. What factors might have influenced these women to speak up?

6. Why do you think these women persisted, even in the face of adversity?

7. Several of these women have been described as having mental health problems. What factors might have contributed to them either actually suffering mental illness or being labeled has having mental health problems?

8. What role did education play in these women's lives? What role did religion play?

9. Although most of these stories took place many years ago, even today, women describe situations in which men have taken credit for their work. What are some of the differences that women today might experience compared to women from a hundred years ago?

10. What would you say to a woman today if she were to tell you that a man took credit for her work? What advice would you offer?

11. Has anyone ever taken credit for your work? How did you respond? Would you respond differently if it were to happen again?

A complete downloadable Reader's Guide
is available from the publisher at
http://www.cynren.com/s/oh-no-he-didnt-guide.pdf.

Index

Q

R

S

WENDY J. MURPHY is an attorney specializing in women's rights, civil rights, constitutional rights, and violence against women and children. Codirector of the Women's and Children's Advocacy Project under the Center for Law and Social Responsibility at New England Law | Boston and a former Visiting Scholar at Harvard Law School, Wendy served as a columnist for the *Boston Herald* for many years and has appeared frequently on network and cable news shows as a pundit and legal analyst. Her first book, *And Justice for Some* (2007), is an exposé of injustices endured by women and children victims of abuse. Wendy, a former child abuse and sex crimes prosecutor, lectures widely on women's rights, Title IX, constitutional law, and criminal justice policy and is a national leader in the fight for the Equal Rights Amendment. A mother of five, a grandmother of one, and a yoga student for life, Wendy lives outside Boston.

Stay in the conversation.

We invite you to join Cynren Press's

Margin Notes

—where we share thoughtful essays, early looks at forthcoming books, and conversations that extend beyond the page.

cynren.com/margin-notes

www.ingramcontent.com/pod-product-compliance
Lightning Source LLC
LaVergne TN
LVHW020043110826
845155LV00029B/610

* 9 7 8 1 9 4 7 9 7 6 4 7 4 *